Discussion Paper Number 16

IMPERIALISM WITH CHINESE CHARACTERISTICS? READING AND RE-READING CHINA'S 2006 DEFENSE WHITE PAPER

NATIONAL INTELLIGENCE UNIVERSITY

WASHINGTON, DC
SEPTEMBER 2011

Michael Metcalf
Faculty, National Intelligence University

Mike Metcalf's discussion paper, *Imperialism with Chinese Characteristics*, argues that China's 2006 Defense White Paper not only explains the importance of China's continuing military buildup but also lays the theoretical foundation of a new defense policy that seems to amount to nothing less than imperialism.

Imperialism with Chinese Characteristics is the 16th book in the NI Press Discussion Paper Series. Discussion Papers highlight aspects of ongoing debates within the Intelligence Community. The goal of the NI Press is to publish high quality, valuable, and timely books on topics of concern to the Intelligence Community and the U.S. government. Books published by the NI Press undergo peer review by senior officials in the U.S. government as well as from civilian academic or business communities.

How to order this book. *Everyone* may download a free electronic copy of this book from our web site at www.NI-U.edu. *U.S. government employees* may request a complimentary copy of this book by contacting us at: press@NI-U.edu. The *general public* may purchase a copy from the Government Printing Office (GPO) at *http://bookstore.gpo.gov*.

Editor, NI Press
Center for Strategic Intelligence Research
National Intelligence University
Defense Intelligence Agency
Joint Base Anacostia-Bolling
Washington, D.C. 20340-5100

Table of Contents

Editor's Note

This unique paper provides two analyses of the 2006 Defense White Paper for the price of one.

First, Metcalf offers an overview of the 2006 Chinese Defense White Paper, considered a landmark document by many China watchers. Next, Metcalf introduces and offers an analysis of Dr. Chen Zhou's analysis of the same White Paper. Dr. Zhou is a researcher in the War Theory and Strategic Studies Department at the People's Liberation Army (PLA) Academy of Military Sciences where he has also served as a principal drafter on all of China's Defense White Papers.

As a bonus feature, the NI Press also includes a U.S. Government English translation of two of Dr. Zhou's articles.

Metcalf writes:

> "The [Chinese] White Papers provide foreign readers a glimpse into China's general mood concerning its current situation as well as a general portrait of China's policies that are designed to protect and further China's interests ... It does appear that, with development becoming the core strategic, and therefore defensive, concern, China's security concern overseas is becoming inseparable from its concern with domestic security. Does this not also raise the prospect that certain military activities overseas might be initiated by China that China might characterize as purely "defensive" because an overseas event was having a unsettling effect on China's domestic stability and security? Might not China consider and portray such initiatives as Just and Legal?"

Whether or not you agree with Mike Metcalf's overall assessment of China's intentions, you will be challenged by this Discussion Paper to think through many important issues.

Cathryn Quantic Thurston, Ph.D.
Editor, NI Press
Director, Center for Strategic Intelligence Research
National Intelligence University

Author's Note

In my reading of the Chinese 2006 Defense White Paper, I found many things unclear - that many important issues could be interpreted many different ways. BUT fortunately, in two articles, Chen Zhou, a primary drafter and coordinator of the White Papers, provides a clear and systematic explanation of what the Paper actually says, and thus, a systematic explanation of China's new Defense Policy.

Chen's explanation reveals a surprisingly expansive Defense Policy caused by the replacement of "Survival" with "Development" as the core of the new state interest and Defense Policy. Chen then describes how this fundamental change leads to important expansive redefinitions of key concepts such as Defensiveness, Comprehensive Security, Just and Legal Use of Force, and Deterrence as well as an extensive enlargement of the scope of the military's missions, the occasions for the use of military power, and an inkling of the capabilities China intends its military to have in the future.

Taken together, the descriptions of the fundamental changes reveal a surprisingly "transparent" picture of China's intentions for its current massive military modernization that includes the eventual acquisition of foreign military bases to support military interventions in various regions of the world in order to protect China's new globalized State Interests.

Author bio: Mike Metcalf holds a BA in Political Science from Western Carolina University, an MA in Political Philosophy from North Carolina State University and a PhD in Political Science from The Catholic University of America. Metcalf worked 25 years at the Defense Intelligence Agency and 5 years at the Department of State's Bureau of Intelligence and Analysis. Over the years, Metcalf has developed a reputation in the intelligence community as a keen study of Chinese intentions. Currently, Mr. Metcalf is teaching at the National Intelligence University, where he focuses on China. This paper grew out of Mr. Metcalf's desire to help students and new analysts learn how to read Chinese documents and make sense of Chinese motivations and intentions.

IMPERIALISM WITH CHINESE CHARACTERISTICS?
READING AND RE-READING CHINA'S
2006 DEFENSE WHITE PAPER

" . . the gravity center of interests has shifted from
survival to development . . ."

INTRODUCTION

China's current "Grand Strategy" has been described as a "transitional" strategy designed to guide China through the coming years as the international system transitions from one of unipolarity to one of multipolarity.[1] We cannot know with certainty to what new strategy China will transition at the end of that process. However, I believe we can infer that new strategy from China's new defense policy (designed to support China's foreign and economic policies in the future) revealed in China's 2006 Defense White Paper.

The paper you are reading argues that China's 2006 Defense White Paper not only explains the importance of China's continuing military buildup but also lays the theoretical foundation of a new defense policy that seems to amount to nothing less than imperialism. It further argues that this change in policy has been brought about primarily by real changes in China's "state interests." These changes have been brought about by China's having entered a new era/stage of development that entails a new relationship to the outside world. This explanation will resolve the seeming paradox that as China's comprehensive national strength continues to increase and as the military threat to China continues to decrease China feels such a powerful need not only to continue but to accelerate the world's largest and most comprehensive military modernization. This paradox is occurring as the international system accelerates toward real multipolarity, as the recent financial crisis in the United States has ordained an eventual decrease in its military budget and lessening of its global influence, and as China seems to skate through the recent international financial crisis.

ON READING CHINESE DEFENSE WHITE PAPERS

China has released a defense white paper every two years since 1998. As one expert on the white papers has described them, "Each PRC white

---

[1] Avery Goldstein, *Rising to the Challenge* (Palo Alto, CA: Stanford University Press, 2005), 38. Also see Evan S. Madeiros, "China's International Behavior: Activism, Opportunism, and Diversification," *Joint Forces Quarterly*, Issue 47, 34–42.

paper has been a 'child of its time' in regard to the context in the preface and the analysis of the security situation in the front of the document."[2] In this sense, the white papers provide foreign readers a glimpse into China's general mood concerning its current situation, as well as a general portrait of China's policies that are designed to protect and further China's interests in that situation. In fact, since these papers are vetted by various components of the Party and State and are not just a reflection of the People's Liberation Army (PLA), it should be seen as having some authoritativeness in other areas such as the economy and diplomacy. In fact, early sections of each paper read more like a product of the Ministry of Foreign Affairs (MFA) (though they are not) than of the PLA, while later sections appear to be exclusive products of the PLA. However, it must be borne in mind that the white paper is also an exercise in public relations and so we should not be surprised that is also reads as an *apologia*—it reveals some things and conceals some things with an eye to producing a reassuring impression of China's policies.[3] In this sense, these white papers should be read carefully and even with a healthy dose of skepticism.

A FIRST READING OF THE 2006 DEFENSE WHITE PAPER

The relevant sections of the 2006 paper are in the first five pages. These sections are the Preface, "The Security Environment," and "National Defense Policy." The paper proceeds in typical Chinese fashion. The Preface gives an enumeration of principles. "The Security Environment" opens with a general overview of the trends, good and bad, at the system, or strategic, level, then does the same at the regional level, and then concludes with good and bad developments in the security environment at large. "National Defense Policy," which we can surmise is a reaction to the security environment, offers a general statement of the policy and then provides six primary characteristics.

Preface

The 2006 Preface pronounces several principles of China's development and security policies. The first principle is that "China pursues a road of peaceful development and endeavors to build a harmonious world of enduring peace and common prosperity."[4] The reason given for such noble concern for the well-being of the rest of the world is that China's

---

2 David Finkelstein, "China's National Defense in 2006 – Roundtable Report," CNA, 2007, 13.

3 Ibid.

4 "China's National Defense in 2006," The Information Office of the State Council, People's Republic of China, 2006, 4.

interests are "bound up with the rest of the world."[5] For this reason, China pursues the interests of both the Chinese people and of the peoples of the world. In keeping with the foregoing, China's *defense* policy aims at two things: securing China's security and unity, and ensuring China's economic development. To the reader, it is not evident whether both aims have equal weight or whether one aim is subservient to the other (it is possible that a new relationship between them has developed). But in the following paragraph we see that China's defense and military modernization is *the requirement* of maintaining China's security and development, but that China will not be a military threat to any other country.[6] Thus we see that China favors all good things, but its continued development as a nation will be dependent on its continuing military development. The reason for this is that China has become closely bound up with the rest of the world, in fact more bound up than at any time in its history. It appears that, for China, interdependence does not necessarily decrease the need for armaments but actually *increases* it, thus contradicting conventional wisdom that economic interdependence decreases the need for military might.

"The Security Environment"

This section of the 2006 Defense White Paper begins by observing that Deng Xiaoping's 1985 assessment that peace and development remain the principal themes of the time remains in effect, but unnamed uncertainties and destabilizing factors are on the increase.[7] At this point the reader might hypothesize that these increasing uncertainties and destabilizing factors will require a sizeable military increase. But what are they?

Global Environment

It appears the requirement for the growth of China's military does not come from military developments on the global level. Indeed, "World peace and security face more opportunities than challenges."[8] The paper continues that major international forces are keeping each other in check, the developing world is becoming stronger, globalization is making rapid progress, and international cooperation on a wide range of issues is increasing. In fact, "all-out confrontations are avoidable for the foreseeable future."[9] But the world is not yet peaceful, and the causes for concern now appear to be produced by globalization. "The impact of globalization

---

[5] Ibid.
[6] Ibid.
[7] Ibid.
[8] Ibid.
[9] Ibid., 5.

3

is spreading into the political, security and social fields."[10] It is not clear why the Chinese view this as cause for concern. Perhaps it means that "Security issues related to energy, resources, finance, information and international shipping routes are mounting."[11] Or perhaps it means something in addition. Nevertheless, there does appear to be one military cause for concern: There seems to be some sort of arms race going on that involves some developed and some developing countries. And apparently the United States has "intensified" alliance activity and threats of force (probably the war on terrorism).

Regional Environment

On the regional level, we also find a mixture of good and bad things. The paper states that the Asia-Pacific region remains stable, the regional economy retains unprecedented momentum, and multilateral activities continue to increase. However, changes in the strategic realignment and relations among major countries, along with increased U.S. attention to the region, seem to threaten stability. Everything else in the region appears to be about the same since the 2004 Defense White Paper.

China's Security Environment

The paper now turns to the security environment proper and declares that China's overall security environment remains sound.[12] Its comprehensive national strength and international standing and influence have increased considerably. China still has security challenges, but it appears these are not of the usual sort. "The growing interconnections between domestic and international factors and interconnected traditional and non-traditional factors have made maintaining national security a more challenging task."[13] This appears to be a new situation, but we cannot say with certainty because we do not know precisely what this means. Nevertheless, it appears to say that, although the military threat to China proper continues to decrease, China will continue its military modernization, perhaps because certain nonmilitary concerns that might require military solutions have arisen. If so, this appears related to a changed connection between domestic and international security and to an equality that has arisen between security concerns and development concerns. China's security strategy ". . . endeavors to enhance both development and security, both internal and external security and both traditional and non-traditional security; works to uphold its sovereignty,

---

[10] Ibid.
[11] Ibid.
[12] Ibid.
[13] Ibid.

unity and territorial integrity and promote national development; and strives to sustain the important period of strategic opportunity for national development."[14] Of particular interest in that quotation is the suggestion that there is a connection between internal security, traditional security, and concern for sovereignty, unity, and territorial integrity on the one hand and between external security, nontraditional security, and national development on the other hand. So now it seems nontraditional concerns for nonterritorial security have been added to the traditional concern for territorial security, and that the new concerns will drive the requirement for military development in the future. At any rate, this section is suggestive but not fully clear.

"National Defense Policy"

"National Defense Policy" is a response to "The Security Environment" and the sometimes ill-defined threats contained therein. But, as we have seen, there are new threats that are not directly related to China's territory or sovereignty. The discussion of the policy begins with a reassurance that China's defense policy remains "purely" defensive in nature and that its primary tasks are to maintain China's security and unity as well as to guarantee its development goals. But, does this not imply that threats to China's development are now seen as threats to China's security and, therefore, that the military now will assume certain missions related to securing economic development—and that these might include certain missions abroad? The paper seems to support this idea by describing the six primary elements of the Defense Policy.

> Principle #1. "Upholding national security and unity, and ensure [sic] the interests of national development . . . It improves its capabilities of countering various security threats, accomplishes diversified military tasks, and ensures that it can effectively respond to crises, maintain peace, deter and win wars under complex circumstances."[15]

This appears to be both the most important paragraph in the paper and also the most enigmatic. On the one hand, it seems to lay out the military missions for which the entire military modernization is intended. On the other hand, we cannot make out clearly exactly what those missions are or the scope or scale of the stage on which the PLA is intended to perform

---

14 Ibid., 5.

15 Ibid. This appears to amount to executing the "historic missions" of the PLA for the new stage in the new century, namely: help maintain ruling position of the CCP; provide a security guarantee for sustaining the period of strategic opportunity; provide a strong support for guaranteeing "national interests"; and, playing a major role in maintaining world peace and promoting mutual development.

them. For example, what are "national interests"? What does it mean to "maintain peace, deter and win wars under complex circumstances"? Do these refer to the ordinary "Taiwan scenario" that for so long has been held by most observers to be the driving force behind China's military modernization (and, by the way, the limit to modernization)? Or does the newly elevated priority given to protecting development extend the scope to include some regional and perhaps extra regional naval missions? Or might the aim be more global in scope? If we view the four historic missions as constituting concentric circles, with preserving the CCP in power the center circle and the others extending outward, we find ever greater geographical scope to each succeeding circle. Then, if we place over these circles the capabilities against "various" security threats enumerated in the last sentence, we might wonder whether capabilities are to be built to allow exercise of these core capabilities in each circle—territorial, regional, and global. I believe it to be the case that we simply do not know the extent of the missions and capabilities discussed in this all-important paragraph.

> Principle #2. "China pursues a coordinated development of national defense and development. It keeps the modernization of China's national defense and armed forces as an integral part of its social and economic development, so as to ensure that the modernization of its national defense and armed forces will advance in step with the national modernization drive."[16]

Once again, these sentences seem to be describing something very important, but we cannot really tell what that is. They do seem to point to a new relationship between economic and military development. In fact, it seems to be pointing to a "circular" relationship in which each depends on the other, and the limit of one will be determined by the limit of the other. This also could have major implications for the size and capabilities of, as well as missions that China now envisions for, its military.

> Principle #3. This section describes the importance of "information-ization" and "mechanization" and "independent innovation" in the modernization of the PLA, and warrants no further discussion.[17]

> Principle #4. This section deals with the expansion of the roles of the PLA in general and with the expansion of the scope and activity of the missions of the branches of the PLA that can be described in a word: outward. "It will upgrade and develop the strategic concept of people's war, and work for the close coordination between military struggle and political, economic, diplomatic, cultural and

---

[16] Ibid, 8.
[17] Ibid.

legal endeavors, uses strategies and tactics in a comprehensive way, and takes the initiative to prevent and defuse crises and deter conflicts and wars."[18] Of course, this section can be interpreted in many ways, but the one thing on which all can agree is that the PLA will become more active and will take the *initiative* in more situations.

Principle #5. This section deals with China's nuclear weapons policy and we must admit that its meaning is somewhat blurry. It assures that China's nuclear strategy is subject to both the state's nuclear policy and its military strategy. After this we have some discussion of the state's nuclear policy but none of its military strategy.

Principle #6. This section describes the many nice things China does on the international stage that contribute to world peace and stability, and it implies that these thing do and will always include only military operations other than war. But, will they?

And thus, we have reached the end of the "theoretical" sections of the white paper and, I hazard to suggest, without a clear understanding of the goals, missions, and capabilities envisioned by China for its military in the "new era." In other words, the important but ambiguous descriptions can be interpreted in many ways, or even in any way we might want. Interpretations can range from the suspicion that something has changed qualitatively and not just quantitatively to the habitual practice of simply adding the most recent events, no matter how unexpected, to last year's list. If only we had access to an authoritative guide to the white paper, perhaps a principal drafter of the paper. Surely he could set us on the right course out of the wilderness. But where could we find such an authoritative guide?

CHEN ZHOU AS OUR GUIDE

Amazingly we have such a guide readily available. Dr. Chen Zhou is a researcher at the PLA Academy of Military Sciences War Theory and Strategic Studies Department and also has served as a principal drafter on all of China's Defense White Papers. In addition, he is one of the most well-known PLA writers on Chinese military matters. Thus, if he were to have written an article that purported to be a commentary on China's 2006 Defense White Paper that provided a cogent description of a new Chinese defense policy that can only be described as revolutionary rather than evolutionary, we might expect it to receive wide attention and thorough analysis. In fact, we got it half right. We gave it wide but brief attention,

---

[18] Ibid.

but apparently not thorough analysis. Perhaps this is because the article requires many readings.

The article in question is titled "An Analysis of Defensive National Defense Policy of China for Safeguarding Peace and Development" and it was published in 2007 by the journal *China Military Science*.[19] The first paragraph of the article contains this sentence: "The 'China's National Defense in 2006' white paper for the first time comprehensively and systematically expounded, in the form of a government document, China's defensive national defense policy in the new stage in the new century." If this is so, it is possible our initial reading of the white paper failed to fully recognize this comprehensive and systematic exposition. Fortunately, however, Chen sets out systematically and comprehensively to expound for us the white paper's meaning.

THE ORGANIZATION OF CHEN'S ARTICLE

Chen's article is arranged by numbered paragraphs, so I shall reference paragraph numbers rather than page numbers. The article is organized as follows: The Preface, in paragraph 2, locates the new policy within the new era; paragraphs 3 through 7 contain a description of the defense policies for different historical periods; paragraphs 8 through 14 contain a discussion of the six basic principles from these historical defense policies; paragraphs 15 - 27 describe the changes in the new Defense Policy to include: in paragraphs 19 and 20, a new judgment of the security environment; in paragraphs 21 and 22, a new definition of "State Interest"; in paragraphs 23 and 24, the new thought on national defense development; and in paragraphs 25 and 26, the development of a new military strategy. Paragraphs 27 through 32 discuss new strategic considerations and new definitions to include: in paragraph 28, a new definition of defensiveness; in paragraph 29, a new expanded definition of comprehensive security; in paragraph 30, a new definition of just and legal use of force; in paragraph 31, new principles of action for the current "transitional" phase; in paragraph 32, an expansion of the definition of deterrence; and, finally, also in paragraph 32, the usual soothing reassurances.

---

[19] A translation entitled, "China: Defensive National Defense Policy" is available on page 27.

Preface.[20] Chen writes that, with changes in the international environment and the elevation of China's comprehensive national strength, China has entered a new development stage. He continues that the new development stage will bring changes in China's security environment, security threats, and challenges. For the moment, I ask the reader to consider that the new Defense Policy can come from changes within China itself rather than changes in other areas; that is, that if the new stage of development entails substantial changes in the way China will interact with the world, then this can be sufficient for a new Defense Policy because those changes can create fundamentally new security threats and challenges. Thus, it is possible China's security threats can increase as the military threat to territorial China decreases.

Defense Policy for different historical periods.[21] This section will sound familiar to most readers so I shall not comment but rather move on to Chen's enumeration of the six basic principles in China's Defense Policies, thus far.

Six Basic Principles of the Defense Policies of Previous Historical Periods [22]

1. **Adhere to the strategic defensive and to the self-defensive military position.**[23] According to Chen, during those past periods the fundamental tasks of national defense had been to "resist aggression, defend the motherland, and protect the peaceful work of the people." Chen continues that this was determined by four things: the state's nature, the state's interests, the foreign policy, and the historical tradition of China. The reader might surmise that change to any of those characteristics (for example, the state's interest) could lead to a modification of the fundamental tasks. However, later we will learn of the fundamental importance Chen gives to the nature of the state and that, so long as this does not change, the fundamental defensiveness of China's defense policy will not change, though the ways it is executed may.

2. **Importance of independence and self-reliance.**[24] This section is rather straightforward and familiar.

---

[20] Paragraph 2.
[21] Paragraphs 3–7.
[22] Paragraphs 8–14.
[23] Paragraph 9.
[24] Paragraph 10.

3. ***Centrality of people's war.***[25] This section appears to be more a formality.

4. ***The relation between military and economic development—adhere to coordinated development.***[26] Chen points out that, historically, China's economic development has been the state's central task, with military construction subject to that interest. Military development must depend on economic development, but military development must keep up with economic modernization. We must wonder what it means for military development that China has reached a new stage in its economic development.

5. ***Adhere to the goal of safeguarding peace.***[27] Chen writes, "Adhering to the goal of safeguarding peace embodies the combination of preserving the nation's security and development with performing our international duties and embodies the nature of the state and the requirements of our domestic and foreign policy."[28] (We shall see later what it means when requirements of preserving the state's security and development are broadened considerably.)

6. ***Adhere to the Party's leadership.***[29] Chen states that maintaining "the CCP's leadership over national defense is the fundamental guarantee for the national security and development."[30]

WHAT'S NEW?

In paragraphs 15 through 18, Chen introduces the foundations of the changes that have produced a new Defense Policy. Basically, according to Chen, the root of the changes is that China has entered a new stage of economic and social development. Based on this, the Party set for itself three historic tasks and Hu Jintao set forth the historic missions the military must accomplish in order that development be fully realized.[31] Chen tells

---

[25] Paragraphs 11.

[26] Paragraphs 12.

[27] Paragraph 13.

[28] Ibid.

[29] Paragraph 14.

[30] Ibid. We might surmise that it is also the fundamental guarantee of the continued unchallenged hold on power by the CCP. This would mean that that continued unchallenged hold on power by the CCP also is a fundamental guarantee of China's security and development.

[31] For a good discussion of the CCP's Historic Tasks and Hu's Historic Missions for the PLA, see Daniel M. Hartnett, "Towards a Globally Focused Chinese Military: The *Historic Missions* of the PLA," CNA, 2008. Hartnett does not push the implications of the Historic Missions as far as I read Chen to do.

us that the 2006 Defense White Paper was based on Hu's declaration of the Historic Missions for the military in the new era. He continues that analyzing "the contents of this policy and its implementation in practice, one may find new changes in the following four aspects."[32]

DOING STRATEGY/POLICY IN A MAOIST/MARXIST CONTEXT

Before examining the four aspects in China's defense policy that have changed, it will be useful to remind ourselves of how Mao Zedong approached the formation of strategy, or, in our case, policy. Two important activities precede the formation of a strategy. First is the determination of the political goal. As Gao Rui tells us, for Mao, "War is the extension of politics . . . It is completely controlled by the politics" so, "the political aim of the war is the basic foundation of military strategy."[33] One might say that the political goal is the end for which the strategy is a means. Therefore, any change in the political goal will necessitate a change in the strategy. The second preliminary activity is to analyze the specific traits, or characteristics, of that particular war. Gao cites Mao saying, "The war has its specific traits due to the difference in time, location, and nature.'"[34] Gao continues, "During the fighting period of the land revolution, Mao Zedong pointed out the basic trait of this war was that it occurred in a large semi-colonial and semi-feudal country in which the political and economical development were greatly lacking balance. The enemy was large, the Red Army was small but led by the Communists and it was a land revolution . . . Thus, the defense strategy became the most important and complex war problem for the Red Army."[35] For our purposes, therefore, I believe we can think of the "trait" as being represented in Chen's article by the "security environment," and of the "political goal" as represented by the "state's interest." So, we must pay close attention to Chen's discussion of the changes in both the security environment and in the state's interest, because the changes will necessitate changes in China's defense policy or strategy.

---

[32] Paragraph 16.

[33] Gao Rui, "The Development and Principles of the Strategic Principles," in Peng Guaqion and Yao Youzhi, eds., *The Science of Military Strategy* (Beijing: Military Science Publishing House, 2001). The article is not paginated. See Section 3, subsection 1, subsection B, "Politics is the soul of military strategy."

[34] Ibid., subsection C, "In formulating strategy, one should focus on the specific trait and development of the war."

[35] Ibid.

THE FOUR CHANGES

1. Change in the security environment.[36] Chen writes that the first important aspect of the defense policy that has changed is the judgment of the security environment, or what Mao would call "the trait." Chen tells us of its importance: "The judgment on the security situation and environment is the prerequisite for formulating the national defense policy."[37] He then proceeds to describe the international situation and then the security environment generally. According to Chen, the international situation is improving with growing interdependence and more movement toward a multipolar order in which the factors supporting peace continue to increase. However, unnamed global challenges and non-traditional threats are increasing and becoming more complex. This change is related to the growing influence of globalization on the international, political, security, social, and cultural spheres. All this can be related to a general rise in the importance of development to become a "core" issue for the international community.[38]

Chen continues that China's security environment is quite favorable, with no real threat of a major war.[39] However, new threats have arisen from the rise of the importance of development for China. In fact, development now affects the overall national security. This is because "Reform and development is now at a critical stage and the contradictions and problems affecting social harmony and stability are increasing. China's economic dependence on the overseas markets is increasing, so the economic security is facing greater risks."[40] The reader can see that, for Chen, security and development seem to be merging into one issue. For example, Chen observes that now the Taiwan problem is no longer merely an issue of national unity but now is also a part of the "anti-containment struggle for guaranteeing the nation's development."[41] And the "containment" policy aimed at China is seen as being as much a threat to development as a threat to territorial security. So, the reader can surmise, because of the rise in the importance of development, not only have new nontraditional threats arisen, but the definitions or natures or essences of old threats can change.

---

[36] Chen, paragraphs 19–20.
[37] Paragraph 19.
[38] Ibid.
[39] Paragraph 20.
[40] Ibid.
[41] Ibid.

2. The new definition of the state's interest.[42] This section reveals the very heart of the matter. It first explains the importance of the state's interest in the formulation of defense policy; second, it explains the enduring importance of the "Marxist" nature of the Chinese state (this issue is fundamental to forming the defense against any charge of imperialism); and third, it elaborates the strategic implications of the rise of the issue of development to the same level as the issues of sovereignty and security.

While the analysis of the security environment was characterized as "prerequisite" to formulation of defense policy, the definition of "state interest," or political goal, is characterized as "the fundamental ground for forming the national defense policy and military strategy."[43] However, Chen quickly points out that China's way of determining the state's interest differs from that of the West, which Chen describes as simply equating it to increased political power. Chen argues that "Marxism holds that social, economic and political relations based on a certain development level of the productive forces determine the existing form of the state interests, and the state interests are the summation of the nation's material and cultural needs and the nation's needs in its survival and development in connection with specific socioeconomic relations."[44] (At this point, let me interject the observation that Marxism is different from a Stalinist economic system: It is a mode of analysis and if one habitually employs that mode of analysis, one is a Marxist. Chen argues that Chinese analysts and planners employ Marxist concepts, categories, and relations, and therefore that they employ Marxist analysis.) Chen believes that because of this Marxist analysis, the development interests have become the "core" of national interests. As he explains it,

> China's national defense always puts the state's sovereignty and security in the primary position, and always takes guarding against and resisting aggression, stopping armed subversion, defending the state's sovereignty, unity, territorial integrity and security as the basic tasks. With the changes of the times and the development of the nation, the security interests and the development interests have been interwoven, the interests of one's own country have been closely linked with the interests of other nations, the gravity center of interests have [sic] shifted from survival to development, the form of realizing the national interests has extended from domestic to

---

[42] Paragraphs 21–22.
[43] Paragraph 21.
[44] Ibid.

international, the scope of the national interests has extended from the traditional territorial land, seas, and air to the maritime, space, and electromagnetic domains . . .[45]

In other words, the new stage of development has caused the merging of development concerns and traditional territorial security concerns, and this has pushed China's state security interests offshore. "Safeguarding the state interests is to preserve the combination of security and development and to guarantee the state's comprehensive security in the political, economic, military and social domains." (What an expansion of missions and scope for the military!) Lest there be any underestimation of the comprehensiveness and scope of the new missions for the military, Chen gives us a series of pairings of military missions and makes it clear that the members of each pair are of equal importance.

> The armed forces need to cope with traditional security threats, and also to cope with non-traditional threats; need to safeguard the state's survival interests, and need to safeguard the state's development interests; need to safeguard the homeland security, and also to safeguard the overseas interests security; need to safeguard the overall state interests of reform, development, and stability, and also need to safeguard world peace and promote common development.[46]

3. New thoughts on national defense development.[47] This section concerns the application of Hu's "scientific development concept" to military development, or to the means of achieving modernization rather than to the ends, which is our concern. Therefore, I shall limit my discussion of this to the observation that it seems to call for faster and more efficient military development.

4. The new development of the military strategy.[48] This section is less specific than we might wish, but it does give us a general idea that military strategy is moving well beyond the Taiwan issue into capabilities against "various security threats" the general outline of which we have seen in previous sections. "The military capability is the core of the state's strategic capability and should be able to be extended to wherever the

---

[45] Paragraph 22.
[46] Ibid.
[47] Paragraphs 23–24.
[48] Paragraphs 25–26.

state's interests develop to."[49] China will be "building a military force commensurate with the state's security and development interests . . ." This will require that the missions of all PLA branches be expanded and extended.[50]

REDEFINITION OF SECURITY CONCEPTS CAUSED BY THE NEW UNDERSTANDING OF THE STATE'S INTEREST

With development becoming the core of the state's interest, all aspects of defense policy and strategy must be brought into conformity with this. As Chen writes, "All our strategic considerations and definitions in carrying out the defensive national defense policy must be unfolded closely around the state's peaceful development strategy."[51] We have already seen how this requirement has expanded the Taiwan issue from one of national unity to also being one of resisting containment of China's development. In this section, we shall see five rather dramatic examples of redefinitions.

Redefinition #1: Defensiveness. "First, understanding the defensiveness of the national defense policy from the political and strategic high plane.[52] Chen states that this means to continue Mao's strategic principle of active defense, or never striking first, because "maintaining the defensiveness . . . is our political superiority, is our core value, and is an important hallmark of the soft power of our state and our armed forces."[53] Chen contrasts China's policy with the Western one he describes as one of strategic offensive and preemptive attack. But it appears China's maintaining that defensiveness and even the appearance of defensiveness will become much more difficult. "Today while the Chinese economy is increasingly merging into the global economic system and the state interests are continuously extending outward, China's national defense will assume a more active and open posture in moving into the outside world, will preserve the state interests in a broader sphere of domains beyond the limits of territory and sovereignty, and will provide military support and guarantee for the development interests."[54] (One might say that, in fact, some of China's future actions could sometimes be indistinguishable from those condemned as characteristic of the West.)

---

[49] Paragraph 26.
[50] Ibid.
[51] Paragraph 27.
[52] Paragraph 28.
[53] Ibid.
[54] Ibid.

From this flows the absolute necessity that China continue to maintain the soft power advantage of a reputation for defensiveness because "in the long run this will greatly boost the just and legal nature of our actions to safeguard the state interests . . ."[55] Thus, though China's actions might appear suspect, this will not be because China has changed but rather because the nature of warfare has changed. "In a local war under the informationized conditions, the difference between strategic, campaign, and tactical actions are fuzzy; the difference between strategic offensive and strategic defense and between striking only after being attacked and striking preemptively will get narrower. These characteristics require that we more flexibly employ the strategy and tactics, give prominence to the offensive operations at the strategic, campaign, and tactical levels, take active offensive actions to seize the strategic initiative and dominance, effectively safeguard the state's security and development interests. This does not change the defensive nature of our national defense policy, but just enrich and develop . . . (it)." The reader will have to form his own opinion of the future status of the "defensive" nature of active defense. But one thing is clear: Chen is at pains to convince the world not to be alarmed by what will appear to be very undefensive behavior by China. This will be discussed more fully later.

Redefinition #2: Broadening the concept of comprehensive security.[56] The implications of merging security and development are further unpacked. "Establishing a scientific security concept with comprehensive security as the core and comprehensively developing and employing the means of national security is the foundation for China's national defense to effectively safeguard the state interests under the new situation. Development and security constitute an organic unified entity, in which development is the foundation of security, and security is the guarantee for development." The reader soon discovers that this means far more than just security needs money and development needs security. It also means there is now a relationship between domestic stability and international developments; that protecting domestic stability now takes on an international dimension.

> China's influence on the international community and the external obstruction that China will be facing will rise side by side, so the domestic security will more heavily influence the international situation and the international security will more deeply influence the domestic situation as well. National defense should coordinate the domestic situation and the international situation, should

---

[55] Ibid.
[56] Paragraph 29.

16

consider and resolve national security issues from the interactive influence of the international and domestic security factors, and should combine the effort to consolidate the internal security with the effort to guard against external threats.[57]

All of this means there is no foreseeable limit to the requirements on and, therefore, the desired capabilities of, the PLA. In fact, we might characterize the security sought as comprehensive, and this means of a very great scope and scale.

> ...with the pace of "stepping out" being quickened, the issue of protecting the overseas interests is getting increasingly prominent. National defense should, from the high plane of economic globalization's development and safeguarding the state's economic security, effectively raise the capability of protecting our country's overseas interests, and ensure the protection of the overseas security while guaranteeing homeland security.[58]

It does appear that, with development becoming the core strategic (and therefore defensive) concern, China's security concern overseas is becoming inseparable from its concern with domestic security. Does this not also raise the prospect of China initiating certain military activities overseas, characterizing them as purely "defensive" because they were undertaken due to an overseas event having an unsettling effect on China's domestic stability and security? Might not China consider and portray such initiatives as just and legal?

Redefinition #3: Safeguarding (expanding) the just and legal nature of the state's interests.[59] Here Chen expands the cover of "just and legal" military action from the traditional territorial security to the international arena. "The international activities aimed at safeguarding the security interests marked by national sovereignty, unity, and territorial integrity are indisputably just in nature . . . The traditional viewpoint holds that 'the physical sphere of national interests is China itself, and can never be extended to other countries and regions.'"[60] But with China's development and economic globalization, "the state's development interests will unavoidably go beyond the scope of the country's territory and will be extended to other countries and regions."[61] And it is here that the inherently "just" nature of the Chinese regime reenters the picture. The "fact" that China is what

---

[57] Ibid.
[58] Ibid.
[59] Paragraph 30.
[60] Ibid.
[61] Ibid.

it is, once again, means that it can be absolved of seemingly unseemly behavior. Chen goes on to assure us that China always will follow "proper procedure" before doing what it has to do in order to protect its interests.[62]

Redefinition #4: Acting according to one's capabilities.[63] In this section we learn that, since China is not yet as militarily strong as it intends to be, it must, for the time being, continue to follow Deng's admonition of "hiding our capabilities and biding our time." So, for the time being, China will be selective in the commitments it undertakes and will continue to take strong positions only on important issues while being more flexible on "ordinary" issues. We must assume that China intends to change this modus operandi as soon as it has sufficient military strength that it no longer must hide and can finally "take the lead" in both important and "ordinary" issues.

Chen concludes this section with the interesting observation that, despite the enduring "security dilemma" China faces, China will not be deterred from increasing its military strength. "How to prevent us from being regarded as a threat because of development and how to prevent us from being self-restrained in development for fear of being regarded as a threat is dilemma that we are facing in the development of national defense."[64] It appears the solution is for China to proceed full-speed-ahead on economic and military development while assuring all concerned that China has only the best of "just and legal" intentions.

Redefinition #5: Deterring wars and crises.[65] This final section deals with building the military capability to deter wars and crises. It is unclear whether this applies only to China, the region around China, or other regions far from China. It appears the addition of "checking" wars (preventing wars that appear imminent) is new and requires more capability than just "winning" wars, with the capability for checking wars being built upon the prior capability to win wars.

FOREIGN MILITARY BASES?

If one is to contend that China intends to become what amounts to an imperial power, one must address the issue of overseas military bases. As is well known, China has until now forthrightly denied that it will station forces abroad or have foreign military bases. But, given that China's

---

[62] Ibid.
[63] Paragraph 31.
[64] Ibid.
[65] Paragraph 32.

national interests are now extending around the globe and that China intends eventually to have the military forces required to protect those interests, the natural test of whether China has "imperial" intentions will be that of foreign military bases. Chen does not address this issue in the article we have just analyzed, but he does in a similar article titled, "China: Defensive National Defense Policy under New Conditions."[66] Toward the end of the article, Chen describes the possible conflict between having a military policy of protecting overseas national interests and both of China's traditional prohibitions against foreign involvement of its military and against interference in other nations' internal affairs. He repeats the argument that, though China must become more involved in other regions of the world, it will never pursue a Western-style policy. "Therefore, though we resolutely oppose 'neo-interventionism' that 'puts human rights above sovereignty,' we cannot negate the overseas use of military for any defensive and humanitarian purposes. We must reserve our right to carry out legal 'intervention' or 'interference' when the nation's core overseas interests are being seriously jeopardized."[67] He continues that military power is the core of national strategic capabilities and that the missions of the military should stretch to wherever the national interests reach. He adds that China's recent participation in UN peacekeeping operations already has broken the proscription against stationing Chinese troops abroad. So, what about foreign military bases? A careful reading of Chen's carefully worded discussion reveals that, in fact, China will have foreign military bases.

> As for whether or not military bases should be established in overseas areas, this is something related to our country's independent peaceful foreign policy and defensive national defense policy, and is also restricted by the national and military conditions, the comprehensive national power, and the path of development of our country . . . These conditions and characteristics and the fact that our military's strength are [sic] not yet commensurate with the requirement of the missions determine that we should act within our capacity in safeguarding our overseas interests, deal with issues case by case, and make steady advances . . . Even when we become really powerful in the future, we will still not establish a global network of military bases on a large scale like some countries do . . . [68]

---

[66] A translation, entitled, "China: Defensive National Defense Policy under New Situation." is available on page 51.

[67] Ibid., paragraph 25.

[68] Chen, paragraph 26.

China will not have overseas bases until it is strong enough nor will the bases imitate the Western model. Rather, China will have a system of overseas bases with (we may infer) Chinese characteristics. A short time ago China foreswore stationing troops abroad and having overseas bases. This appears to have been determined purely by China's weakness. In the future, China will not be weak and will therefore (we may again infer) behave like a strong country. It certainly appears that any assurances given today that China's behavior in the future will not mimic "Western" behavior should be given the same credence we now give past claims that China would never station troops abroad or have foreign military bases. Thus, as China's power increases, its behavior and rhetoric also change.

CHINA TODAY AS THE LAND OF "NOT YET"

What is the best method for interpreting China's current military and strategic behavior? We observe it closely every day, but in what context should we place the behavior? Leaving aside the merely behavioral approach, it appears we have two perspectives: seeing it as an extension of the past or seeing it as a preparation for the future. If we choose to see current China's activity as no more than an add-on to last year's activity, we run the risk of missing the early stages of fundamental changes as well as the risk of seeing the future goals as merely additions to past goals.

An alternative perspective would resemble the teleological explanation that sees activity in light of the end at which it aims. For example, were one to attempt to describe an acorn, one might say that it falls from a tree in the autumn and that it is composed of certain minerals in certain proportions. But to truly understand an acorn one must see it in the light of what it might become, namely a mighty oak. One might say the oak—the purpose, or the goal—pulls the acorn forward and gives it its fullest meaning. Thus, to fully appreciate present Chinese behavior, it must be seen from the perspective of the future at which it aims. I believe that Chen's explanation of the 2006 Defense White Paper gives us that goal: a very powerful China active in the international arena, using its military strength to further and protect its interests and diplomacy, and with a series of military bases abroad to support those military missions. In other words, they intend imperialism with Chinese characteristics.

So, can we explain China's current behavior by using this perspective? I believe we can by seeing China currently as the "Country of Not Yet" that must continue to hide its strength and bide its time until such time as it will no longer need to. As Chen puts it, "China is a large developing country that is getting richer but not affluent yet, and getting stronger but not powerful yet. We must adhere to the strategic principle of hiding our capabilities and biding our time for making accomplishments over time."[69] Therefore, according to Chen, China is in the process of laying the foundation for the military it will need *in the future* in order to carry out its historic missions:

> Therefore we should continue to emancipate the mind, seek truth from facts, actively explore the forms and methods of carrying out our military's overseas military actions . . . We should quickly raise the armed forces' rapid response, strategic delivery, and comprehensive support capabilities . . . We should expand the sphere of maritime activity, strive to demonstrate our presence in some critical strategic regions, use diplomatic and economic means to establish strategic supporting points, and make use of berthing points and supply points to which we legally get access from relevant countries in the relevant sea areas. We should, according to the strategic requirement of getting needed support, explore new forms of military security cooperation beyond the scope of general exchange. We should quicken the pace of establishing a legal system for foreign military actions . . .[70]

These all are things that a short time ago we would not have seen, yet also things that China is doing in *the meantime* until it has achieved the desired level of military strength. At that time, when China acts according to its capabilities, it will pursue goals for which the above is but preparation.

CONCLUSION

The state's interest is the foundation of China's security and defense policies. The center of gravity of China's state interest has changed from China's survival to China's development. Therefore, the primary mission of China's military is no longer China's survival and territorial security but now is protecting and expanding China's developmental interests, wherever those interests might be located. This mission will require a much greater military force than was required when mere survival and territorial defense formed the core of China's state interest. Let us recall that, for Mao, the first objective of the commander of a weak army is its survival—a strategy of active defense. Only after he had increased his own strength and weakened his opponent's strength could he adopt new modes and strategies—once

---

[69] Ibid.
[70] Ibid.

survival has been assured, the goal can change from survival to victory. So, the core of China's state interest has changed from mere survival to development—and this is a major event. It is a qualitative change and not a mere quantitative change. China has crossed a threshold.

Not long ago it was possible to reach a loose consensus on what military force China would require and develop. When survival was the primary objective, people's war could provide defense against a conventional invasion of China but not against a nuclear attack. Once China deployed a small but reliable nuclear force, China had assured its survival. The only remaining issue was territorial reunification and this would require new military capabilities beyond those of mere survival. But, one still could imagine a limit to the size and capabilities of a force capable of securing Taiwan and the South China Sea. This, however, is no longer the case. With development as the new core of state interest, the only limit to China's military needs will be the limit of China's development interests. But development interests seem to be of a type that constantly expands. Or is China of such a nature that one day it will declare that its development has reached its desired limit?

Unless one can predict the limit of China's development goals, one cannot predict the limit of China's military requirement. China plans to develop a military force commensurate with its economic status, with most analysts assessing that its status will surpass that of the United States by earlier than mid-century. But will China then stop? At present its military development lags behind even its current requirement. Therefore, for a very long time China's military development will be racing not only to catch up to its current requirement but also to prepare for future requirements that have no foreseeable limits.

BIBLIOGRAPHY

Finkelstein, David. "China's National Defense in 2006 – Roundtable Report." Alexandria, VA: CNA, 2007.

Chen Zhou. "China: Defensive National Defense Policy under New Situation." Defense Department translation. *China Military Science*, (6) 2009.

Chen Zhou. "China: Defensive National Defense Policy." 2007. Defense Department translation. China Military Science, (6) 2007.

Gao Rui, "The Development and Principles of the Strategic Principles," in Peng Guaqion and Yao Youzhi, eds. *The Science of Military Strategy.* Beijing: Military Science Publishing House, 2001.

Goldstein, Avery. *Rising to the Challenge.* Palo Alto, CA: Stanford University Press, 2005.

Hartnett, Daniel M. "Towards a Globally Focused Chinese Military: The Historic Missions of the PLA." Alexandria, VA: CNA, 2008.

Information Office of the State Council, People's Republic of China. "China's National Defense in 2006." 2006.

Madeiros, Evan S. "China's International Behavior: Activism, Opportunism, and Diversification," *Joint Forces Quarterly,* Issue 47.

An Analysis of Defensive National Defense Policy of China for Safeguarding Peace and Development

By Dr. Chen Zhou, *China Military Science*, (6) 2007, pages 1-10

A full text translation follows.

TEXT:

1. **Abstract:** China's national defense policy in the new stage of the new century maintains and develops the basic thoughts and principles of national defense policy pursued by New China in its different historical periods, gives prominence to the status of the scientific development concept as the guiding idea for the national defense policy, and seeks to build up strong and solid national defense with a view to safeguarding peace, development, and the overall national interests. This policy, which is commensurate with the changes in the general domestic and international situation, gives full expression to the new judgment of the party's Central Committee and the Central Military Commission on the security environment, the new definition of national interests, the new thought on national defense development, and the new development of the military strategy. To adhere to the complete strategic thinking on and definition of the defensive national defense policy, we must unfold the work in close connection with the overall interests of the state's peaceful development strategy.

2. With the progress of the times, the changes of the security environment, and the elevation of the comprehensive national power, China has stepped into a new development stage in the new century with a more self-confident and more self-strengthening posture of being open and active. The "China's National Defense in 2006" white paper for the first time comprehensively and systematically expounded, in the form of a government document, China's defensive national defense policy in the new stage of the new century. This policy maintains and develops the basic thoughts and principles of the national defense policy of New China in its different historical periods, is commensurate with the new changes of the contemporary domestic and international situation, complies with and serves the state's development strategy and security strategy, seeks to build up strong and solid national defense with a view to safeguarding peace, development, and the overall national interests. It gives concentrated expression to the national defense strategic thinking and practical activity of the party Central Committee with Comrade Hu Jintao as general secretary, and charts a clear course for us to quicken the process of national defense and armed forces modernization under the new historical conditions.

3. **(I) The Historical Development of New China's National Defense Policy.** National defense provides security guarantee for a country's survival and development. In the different historical periods since the founding of New China, the CPC leaders in several generations formulated, implemented, and adjusted the national defense policy in good time according to the changes in the security situation and the requirements of national defense, thus continuously enhancing the construction of national defense, ensuring the reasonable and effective use of the defense forces, flexibly coping with various security threats and challenges, and giving full play to the role of national defense as the pillar for preserving national sovereignty, security, and interests.

4. The founding of New China marked the beginning of a new period for consolidating national defense, safeguarding the new government, and guaranteeing peaceful construction after our party led the people's army to fight bloody wars for 22 years. At that time, national security was facing domestic trouble and foreign invasion. In particular, there existed the actual threats of large-scale foreign invasion. The domestic reactionary force joined hands with the international anti-China force in attempting to strangle the new government in China in the cradle. China adopted the foreign policy of "leaning to one side," that is, leaning to the socialist camp headed by the Soviet Union, provided foreign military aid by entering into the War to Resist US Aggression and Aid Korea and the military actions of supporting Vietnam in fighting against French colonialists, and carried out a series of military operations from liberating Yijiangshan Island, bombarding Jinmen, to quenching the Tibetan rebellion. Mao Zedong explicitly laid down the strategic task of building strong army, navy, and air force, and realizing the modernization of national defense, and also decided to develop our own atomic bombs, hydrogen bombs, and manmade satellites. In March 1956, the Central Military Commission officially established the positive defensive strategic principle for defending the motherland on the basis of coping with possible sudden strategic attacks by the armed forces headed by the US forces on the eastern coastal area of our country. In January 1960, the Central Military Commission set forth the strategic principle of "resistance in the north and opening the door in the south," and stressed that different operation guidance be given to the northern and southern battlefronts in the eastern coastal area. In this stage, the core of the national defense policy was to consolidate national defense, oppose aggression, entering into alliance with the Soviet Union, and striving for peace.

5. In the 1960s and 1970s, the security situation became sterner. The United States launched a war of aggression against Vietnam, and continued to threaten China from the east and the south. With the rupture of relations between China and the Soviet Union, the Soviet Union deployed over 100

million troops along the Sino-Soviet and Sino-Mongolian borders, and posed threats against China from the north. Beginning from the mid-1960s, China began to shift the focus of its defense policy and military strategy to the basic point of getting ready to fight a large-scale war at an earlier date and even fighting a nuclear war. In those years, China was prepared to cope with the simultaneous attacks from the imperialists, the revisionists, and the reactionaries, and was ready to fight in two or more fronts at the same time. Luring the enemy forces into deep rear areas became the center part of the military strategy. From the beginning of the 1970s, the Soviet Union posed serious threats against China in the three directions of north, west, and south. Mao Zedong then put forth the "one line" strategic thought of establishing an international united front to jointly struggling against the Soviet hegemony. The key points of the military strategy was to resist the Soviet Union's large-scale invasion. The main strategic directions were set to Northeast China, Northern China, and Northwest China, and the main defensive direction is set to Northern China. In 1977, the Central Military Commission adopted the strategic principle of "active defense, luring the enemy in deep," stressed that in the initial stage of war, it would be necessary to stop the enemy from driving straight in, and then luring the enemy in deep to the pre-set battlefields for annihilation. In this period, the state work was focused on the construction of national defense. The nationwide war preparation work was unfolded. The pace of developing weapons and armaments was quickened. We successfully developed and tested atomic and hydrogen bombs and launched manmade satellites in this period. The Second Artillery was established. The PLA carried out military struggle in the southeast coastal areas, carried out self-defensive counterattack operations in Sino-Indian border areas, on Zhenbao Island, and on Xisha Islands, and carried out military actions in supporting Vietnam and Laos against US aggression. The major adjustment of the national defense policy was of positive significance in preventing the possible full-scale war of aggression against China through effective deterrence. However, as the country stayed over a long time in a state of being on high alert to the possible war by making constant military mobilization, this also affected economic development and the long-term development of the armed forces.

6. From the late 1970s to the 1980s, the international situation was eased up. Deng Xiaoping made the basic judgment that peace and development were the theme of the times, changed the viewpoint that the war may break out instantly and the "one-single-line" diplomatic strategy, resolutely shifted the center of the state's work to economic construction. Thus, a major change occurred in China's national defense policy. In the early 1980s, according to the features of the future full-scale anti-aggression

war, the Central Military Commission changed the strategic principle of active defense and luring the enemy in deep into "active defense", and laid down the strategic guiding principles of gaining dominance by striking after the enemy's attacks on us, holding to the people's war, fighting protracted warfare, fighting in a way of defeating superior enemy forces with weaker forces, and being ready to fight in complicated and difficult conditions. In 1985, a strategic change was made in the guiding thought for military forces building. The state of constantly being on high alert and being ready to fight a large-scale war or even a nuclear war at an earlier date was really changed to the state of peaceful construction. The building of military forces was centered at effecting modernization in a planned and orderly way on the basis of being subject to the overall interests of the state's economic construction. In 1988, the Central Military Commission reestablished the military strategy of active defense, stressed the need to change the strategic guideline from getting ready to resist the enemy large-scale invasion at any time to mainly coping with possible local wars and military conflicts, gradually improve the strategic situation in the southern front on the basis of basically stabilizing the strategic posture in the north, attach greater importance to maritime defense and to defending and safeguarding the state's maritime rights and interests, and raise the real battle fighting capability and overall deterring capacity of the armed forces. In this period, the PLA carried out the self-defensive counterattack operation in the Sino-Vietnamese border areas and the sea battles in the Nansha area, downsized the forces by cutting off 1 million troops, and carried out comprehensive structural and organizational readjustments and reforms. In this period, the objective of the national defense policy was mainly to safeguard national interests and the peaceful environment, be subject to and serve the overall interests of economic construction, get ready to cope with local wars and military conflicts, and boost the building of military forces with modernization as the central link.

7. From the beginning of the 1990s, the world's bipolar pattern was dissolved and the international situation in general continued to ease up, but there existed a serious imbalanced condition in the comparison of international strength. On the basis of profoundly understanding the international strategic pattern, the changes in China's security environment, and the development in the world's new revolution in military affairs, Jiang Zemin made a major adjustment of the national defense policy and the military strategy. In 1993, the Central Military Commission formulated the military strategic principle for the new period, and decided to put the basic point of the military struggle preparations to winning local war to be fought with modern technologies, especially high technologies, and to shift the gravity center of the strategy from the "three north" aspects to

the southeast coast aspect. The new military strategic principle stressed the necessity of accelerating the quality building of the armed forces and raising the emergency operation capability, and the focal point was to prevent the occurrence of a major "independence" event in Taiwan. In 1995, the Central Military Commission explicitly set forth the strategy of relying on science and technology for strengthening the armed forces, and required that a change be made in force building from a quantity and scale pattern to a quality and efficiency pattern and from a manpower-intensive pattern to a technology-intensive pattern. After the beginning of the new century, the Central Military Commission further decided to put the basic point of the military struggle preparations to winning local war in informatized conditions, and required that efforts be made actively to advance the revolution in military affairs with Chinese characteristics. The PLA enhanced the building of the Navy, the Air Force, and the Second Artillery as the main parts of the combat forces, quickened the pace of weapon and armament modernization, twice downsized the forces by a total of 700,000 troops, established a national defense mobilization that was suited to the requirements of modern warfare, and organized a series of military deterring actions against Taiwan. In this period, the objective of the national defense policy was mainly to safeguard the nation's security and unity, promote the coordinated development of national defense construction and economic construction, build up the capability of winning high-tech and informatized warfare, make military struggle preparations against "Taiwan independence," and advance the revolution in military affairs with Chinese characteristics.

8. By recalling the development of China's national defense policy over more than half a century and analyzing the features of the national defense policy in different historical periods, we may sum up following six basic principles of common significance:

9. First, adhere to strategic defense. No matter how the environment, the interests, and the actual strength change, China's national defense policy is always defensive in nature, and always strictly adheres to the self-defensive position militarily, without trying to take any preemptive action, without making overseas aggression and expansion and seeking hegemony. The fundamental task of national defense is to resist aggression, defend the motherland, and protect the peaceful work of the people. This is determined by the state nature, the state interests, the foreign policy, and the historical tradition of this country. The military strategic principle of active defense has the same origin as the defensive national defense policy does, both adhering to strategic defensiveness, self-defense, striking only after the enemy strikes, and honoring the tenet that "we will not attack unless we are attacked, if we are attacked, we will certainly counterattack." However,

such defensiveness is a kind of active defense, it combines the principle of strategic defense and striking only after being attacked with that of offensive actions and seizing preemptive opportunities to conquering the enemy in campaigns and battles, and it is the combination of adhering to the defensive nature of the national defense policy with the firmness in defending the state interests.

10. Second, adhere to independence and self-determination. Being independent and self-determining is the core of China's peace diplomatic policy, and also a basic principle in China's national defense policy and national defense modernization drive. In such a large country with a huge population as China, national defense must be constructed and consolidated mainly with the domestic forces independently in a self-reliant way. China never enters into alliance with any large countries or groups of countries, never participates in any military camps, and will independently handles everything concerning national defense and security. China always makes its own strategic judgments according to the rights and wrongs in each event on the basis of the fundamental interests of the Chinese people and the world's people, and formulates its own defense policy and military strategy according to the actual conditions of the country and the armed forces by itself. China constantly relies on its own efforts in building the defense industry and the defense science and technology system, independently develops its own national defense theory and military theory with its own characteristics. When the national security is being threatened or endangered, China persistently relies on its own strength to safeguard its national security and interests.

11. Third, adhere to the entire people's self-defense. China's national defense is all-out defense. The people constitute the most profound source of the strength for national defense. Upholding and developing the strategic thought of the people's war, relying on the broadest masses of people in constructing and consolidating national defense, organizing the entire people's self-defense represent China's real superiority and strength. The national defense policy and the military strategy of New China were all established on the basis of the people's war and the entire people's self-defense. While facing new changes in modern warfare, China maintains the combination of the crack standing forces with the strong national defense reserve forces. While enhancing the building of the armed forces, China also attaches great importance to the building of the militia and reserve forces; continuously adjusts and improves the national defense mobilization system and raises the national defense mobilization capacity in accordance with the principle of effecting peacetime-and-wartime combination, effecting military-and-civilian combination, and embedding military strength in the civilian sector; creates new battle methods that are

suited to the people's participation in battles under modern conditions so as to give play to the overall power of the people's war.

12. Fourth, adhere to coordinated development. Developing the economy and strengthening national defense are always two major strategic tasks in China's modernization. The state constantly takes economic construction as the central task, so national defense construction must be subject to and serve this overall interest, and must closely support this overall interest of the nation. In the meanwhile, the state must advance the modernization of national defense on the basis of economic development, build up military strength in keeping with the nation's economic strength and in keeping with the needs in safeguarding national security, and establish mechanisms for ensuring the reciprocal promotion of coordinated development of national defense construction and economic construction. The armed forces must enhance quality building, and always adhere to the course of relying on science and technology for strengthening, managing the troops on the basis of laws and regulations, building crack troops with Chinese characteristics; must rely on the state's economic and technological development, raise the level of scientific management, take the modernization course of less input and higher efficiency; must actively and prudently advance reforms in all fields, effect the coordinated development of the combat forces, and take a course of compound and leapfrog development.

13. Fifth, adhere to the goal of safeguarding peace. Safeguarding world peace and opposing aggression and expansionist behavior is always an important objective and task of China's national defense. The achievements in China's revolution and construction cannot do without the support from the world's people. China's future is closely linked to the world's future. China's national defense has close relation with the world's peace. Adhering to the goal of safeguarding peace embodies the combination of preserving the nation's security and development with performing our international duties, and embodies the nature of the state and the requirements of our domestic and foreign policy. China opposes hegemonism and power policies; opposes the war policy, the aggression policy, and the expansionist policy; opposes any arms race; supports all activities that are favorable to preserving world and regional peace, security, and stability. China persistently upholds the five principles of peaceful coexistence, develops military cooperative relations that do not enter into any alliance, do not cause confrontation, and do not target at any third party, actively takes part in foreign military exchange and cooperation, and strives to create a military security environment marked by mutual trust and mutual benefit.

14. Sixth, adhere to the party's leadership. Maintaining the CPC's leadership over national defense is the fundamental guarantee for the

national security and development. Maintaining the party's absolute leadership over the armed forces is a primary principle for the building of the people's armed forces. After the founding of New China, maintaining the party's absolute leadership over the armed forces came into line with the state's leadership over the armed forces. The same Central Military Commission is set up for both the party and the state, with exactly the same membership and exactly the same functions of leading the armed forces. That is the same body with two name boards. The fundamental system of the party's leadership over the armed forces is effected through the unified collective leadership of party committees (party branches) in all military units through the responsibility and division-of-work system among leaders. The provincial military districts, military sub-districts, the people's armed force departments, and the reserve force units are subject to the dual leadership of the military system and the local party committees. This system not only guarantees the party's absolute leadership over the armed forces, but also facilitates the operation of the state apparatus in comprehensively enhancing national defense and military force building.

15. **(II) New Changes in the National Defense Policy in the New Stages of the New Century.** The new stage of the new century is not only marked by changes in the times and the situation, but is also determined by the features of a stage of economic and social development. The fifth plenary session of the 15th CPC Central Committee in October 2000 pointed out for the first time that from the beginning of the new century, our country would enter a new development stage of building a well-off society in an all-round way and quickening the process of socialist modernization. The 16th CPC National Congress in November 2002 further emphasized the necessity of seizing the important strategic opportunity period of national development, striving to achieve the objective of building a well-off society in an all-round way in the new stage of the new century. Since the beginning of the 21st century, the international situation has been undergoing profound changes. When facing the pressure of the changing situation, a nation may just retrogress if failing to make new progress. Our country has successfully accomplished the first and second steps in the "three step" strategy for modernization, and has begun to enter the development stage of accomplishing the third-step strategic objective of building a well-off society in an all-round way in the process of modernization.

16. Under the new historical conditions, our party set forth the three major historical tasks of further advancing the process of modernization, accomplishing the motherland's reunification, safeguarding world peace and promoting common development. To guarantee the fulfillment of the strategic development task and the party's historical tasks in the new stage of the new century, Comrade Hu Jintao explicitly set forth the historical

mission for the PLA in the new stage of the new century, that is, to provide important strength guarantee for the party to consolidate the governing status, to provide strong security guarantee for the important strategic opportunity period of national development, to provide effective strategic support for safeguarding the national interests, and to play an important role in safeguarding world peace and promoting common development. He required that the scientific development concept be taken as an important guiding principle for the construction of national defense and for the building of military forces, and be consciously implemented in all aspects and in the whole process of national defense and armed forces construction.

17. On the basis of Comrade Hu Jintao's important thoughts about national security, national defense, and the building of the armed forces, the "China's National Defense in 2006" white paper gave a comprehensive and systematic exposition on China's defensive national defense policy in the new stage of the new century. It announced to the world that the Chinese government, by combining the fundamental interests of the Chinese people and the common interests of all peoples in the world, resolutely pursues a defensive national defense policy; China's national defense is subject to and serves the state's development strategy and security strategy, is aimed at preserving the national security and unity and guaranteeing the achieving of the grand objective of building a well-off society in an all-round way. The main contents of the national defense policy in the new stage of the new century are: Safeguard national security and unity, preserving the nation's development interests; ensure the comprehensive, coordinated, and sustainable development of national defense and armed forces construction; enhance the quality building of the armed forces with informatization as the main hallmark; implement the military strategic principle of active defense; adhere to the nuclear strategy of self-defense; create a security environment favorable to peaceful development of the nation.

18. The national defense policy in the new stage of the new century gives full expression to the basic concept of China's national defense for safeguarding peace and development, gives prominence to the guiding status of the scientific development concept in the national defense policy. Deeply analyzing the contents of this policy and its implementation in practice, one may find new changes in the following four aspects.

19. The new judgment on the security environment. The judgment on the security situation and environment is the prerequisite for formulating the national defense policy. The contemporary world is situated in a period of major changes and adjustments. Peace and development remain the theme

of the times. The world's multi-polarization and economic globalization trend is still developing in depth. The serious imbalanced condition in the comparison of international strategic strength is being improved. The interdependent interest relations among various countries are continuously getting deeper. The big power relationship marked by both competition and cooperation is getting more salient. Russia is quickening the pace of its regeneration, and is struggling with Europe and the United States with a tougher posture. The general strength and international influence of the European Union are increasing, and the European Union is trying to play a greater role in the international community. Japan is seeking the status as a big power, and assumes a more obviously aggressive posture. Various rising developing big countries are quickening their development, and the overall strength of the developing countries is rising. After the "9/11" incident, the United States gave prominence to anti-terrorism, prevention of proliferation, and guarding against challenges from other big powers. As a result, however, the situation in Iraq and Afghanistan continued to get worse; the issue of nuclear proliferation became more outstanding. The factors of safeguarding peace, restraining war, and containing the hegemony are continuously increasing. It is not possible that a large-scale war may break out over a fairly long period of time. The situation with the coexistence of peace and stability with local conflicts on the whole will continue and develop. In view of the world as a whole, though the issue of peace remains, the issue of development has risen to be a core issue for the international community. New global challenges are increasing; non-traditional security threats have become more salient; the struggle between a unipolar world pattern and a multi-polar world pattern will mainly be reflected in the trial of comprehensive national strength; the economic globalization has deeply influenced the international economic, political, security, social, and cultural spheres; the security threats are getting increasingly comprehensive, diverse, and complicated.

20. China's security environment on the whole is favorable, and there is no instant danger of large-scale foreign aggression against China. China's comprehensive national strength and international influence continue to increase. China also continuously develops pragmatic cooperation with major powers, friendly and good-neighborly relations with peripheral countries, and comprehensive exchange with other developing countries. From the angle of long-term development, the issue of sovereignty and national unification remains grave, but the issue of development has risen to one that affects the overall situation of national security. Reform and development in China is now in a critical stage, and the contradictions and problems affecting social harmony and stability are increasing. China's economic dependence on the overseas markets is increasing, so

the economic security is facing greater risks. The threats from the "three forces" with connection inside and outside the country are gradually getting more salient. Terrorist incidents have more frequently occurred in the peripheral areas. The "Taiwan independence" separatist force and its activity constitute the currently largest threat to the state security. The struggle around the Taiwan issue is not only the anti-division struggle for guaranteeing the state's security and unity, but also the anti-containment struggle for guaranteeing the nation's development.

21. The new definition of the state interests. In the late 1970s, China's state strategy made a major change, that is, it consistently took the state interests as the supreme norm for handling affairs and formulating policies, and no longer took ideologies and social systems as a criteria for drawing a line of demarcation. The state interests became the fundamental starting point and also final end of formulating all strategies and policies by the state. The safeguarding of the state interests is the fundamental ground for forming the national defense policy and the military strategy. The Western theory about international politics always puts the state interests on a par with political powers. However, Marxism holds that social economic and political relations based on a certain development level of the productive forces determine the existing form of the state interests, and the state interests are the summation of the nation's material and cultural needs and the nation's needs in its survival and development in connection with specific socioeconomic relations. Only according to this point of view can we really understand the state's fundamental interests in our country's reform, opening up and in the process of our socialist modernization, that is to "safeguard the state's sovereignty, unity, territorial integrity, and security; keep economic construction as the central task, continuously raise the comprehensive national power; maintain and improve the socialist system; maintain and promote social stability and unity; strive for a long-lasting peaceful international environment and a benign peripheral environment." (The Information Office of the PRC State Council: "China's National Defense in 2002," December 2002)

22. China's national defense always puts the state's sovereignty and security in the primary position, and always takes guarding against and resisting aggression, stopping armed subversion, defending the state's sovereignty, unity, territorial integrity, and security as the basic tasks. With the changes of the times and the development of the nation, the security interests and the development interests have been interwoven, the interests of one's own country have been closely linked with the interests of other nations, the gravity center of interests has shifted from survival to development, the form of realizing the national interests has extended from domestic to international, the scope of the national interests has extended from

the traditional territorial land, seas, and air to the maritime, space, and electromagnetic domains, and the development interests have become the core of national interests. According to the long-term strategic interests of the state, Comrade Hu Jintao explicitly raised the state's development interests to the same important position as security interests, and emphasized that national defense "should put the tasks of safeguarding the state sovereignty, security, territorial integrity, and guaranteeing the state's development interests in a position above anything else;" in the new stage of the new century, the fundamental focal point of the historical mission for the armed forces is to "safeguard the state sovereignty, security, and unity, and guarantee the state's development interests". ("Readers for Theoretical Study on Establishing and Implementing the Scientific Development Concept", pp 133, 163, Beijing, the PLA Press, 2006) The armed forces need to cope with traditional security threats, and also need to cope with non-traditional security threats; need to safeguard the state's survival interests, and also need to safeguard the state's development interests; need to safeguard the homeland security, and also need to safeguard the overseas interests security; need to safeguard the overall state interests of reform, development, and stability, and also need to safeguard world peace and promote common development. Safeguarding the state interests is to preserve the combination of security and development and to guarantee the state's comprehensive security in the political, economic, military, and social domains.

23. The new thoughts of national defense development. The nation's development needs to follow the guidance of the scientific development concept, the development of national defense also needs to comprehensively implement the scientific development concept, with efforts being made to effect scientific development. "The primary tenet of the scientific development concept is development, its core is people-centered, its basic requirement is comprehensive, coordinated, and sustainable development, and its fundamental method is overall planning and across-the-board coordination." ("Hu Jintao's speech at the advanced study class of cadres at the provincial and ministerial level at the Central Party School," 26 June 2007) The requirement of the scientific development concept is development, is high-quality and high-efficiency development. On the basis of making quicker developments in national defense and military force building, the key to implementation of the scientific development concept lies in ensuring the development is healthy and fast, and seeking rapidity while first guaranteeing the healthiness of the development. The development of national defense and military forces must be based on a change in the development concept, on the innovation of the development mode, on the enhancement of the development quality, and on scientific

planning, scientific organization, and scientific implementation, with the limited military funds being properly managed and used so as to really effect comprehensive, coordinated, and sustainable development.

24. The main contents of the scientific development of national defense and military forces include the following points: First, generally coordinate the national development and the development of national defense. To ensure the coordinated development of national defense construction and economic construction under the new situation, it is necessary to consider and design the development strategy for national defense and the armed forces from the high plain of the national development strategy, deeply embed the modernization of national defense and military forces in the economic and social development system, comprehensively promote the military-and-civilian combination in the economic, scientific and technological, educational, and human resources aspects, create a favorable situation for the sharing and mutual transfer of high technologies between the military and civilian sectors. Second, properly coordinate the work in various aspects inside the armed forces. It is necessary to enhance the comprehensive building of the armed forces, persist in rigorously managing the troops on the basis of laws and regulations, give play to the main entity role of the troops, advance the work in the military, political, logistic, and armament departments in a well-coordinated way, scientifically coordinate the revolution in military affairs with Chinese characteristics with the preparations for military struggle, coordinate the mechanization efforts with the informatization efforts, coordinate the building of combat strength in various services and arms, coordinate current construction with long-term development, and coordinate construction in the main strategic direction with construction in other strategic directions. Third, rely on scientific and technological progress to effect the change of the fighting capacity generation mode. It is necessary quicken the quality building of the armed forces with informatization as the hallmark, raise the independent innovation capability in armament development and in national defense science and technology, enhance the systems integration among all services and arm branches, promote the change of military training from a mechanized condition to an informatized condition, cultivate high-quality new-type military personnel who are suited to the needs in informatized warfare. Fourth, carry forward the military organizational and structural innovation and the military management innovation. It is necessary to deepen the adjustments and reforms of the organizational structure and the policies and systems, lay stress on resolving the deep-level contradictions and problems that have become structural hindrances to the development of the armed forces, enhance strategic planning and scientific management, improve the top-level designs, explore the

scientific management model with the unique characteristics of our armed forces, and effect the combination of speed, quality, and efficiency in the development of the armed forces.

25. The new development of the military strategy. The changes in the international situation, in the security environment, and in the military struggle tasks, the obvious increase in the comprehensiveness, interrelatedness, overall effects, and suddenness of the national security issues, and the closer relations of military struggle with political, economic, diplomatic, cultural, and legal affairs have all raised higher requirements for the military strategy. The military strategy must plan and guide military actions from the political high plane and from the overall state interests, must be based on a broader strategic vision, must pay closer attention to the national development, and must be subject to and serve the state's general development strategy. In the making of military struggle preparations, in the building of the armed forces in various aspects, and in major military actions, "it is all necessary to give consideration to, and make plans in accordance with, the requirement of safeguarding the important strategic opportunity period and safeguarding the overall state interests" ("Readers for Theoretical Study on Establishing and Implementing the Scientific Development Concept", p 74). The military strategic principle for the new period not only aims at winning local war in informatized conditions, but also requires the comprehensive use of various means and policies to prevent and resolve crises, and to check the outbreak of conflicts and wars; not only requires that a good job be done in the military struggle preparations against "Taiwan independence" and in other aspects, but also requires that good preparations be made to cope with various security threats; not only requires the enhancement of the fighting capability in real war under the informatized conditions, but also requires the enhancement of the strategic deterring strength.

26. The military capability is the core of the state's strategic capability, and should be able to be extended to wherever the state's interests develop to. The military strategy should play an active role in advancing the revolution in military affairs with Chinese characteristics, in quickening the process of achieving the strategic objective of building informatized forces and winning informatized warfare, and in building a military force commensurate with the state's security and development interests; it should attach importance to planning and guiding the non-war actions of the armed forces, take initiative in advancing international military security cooperation, actively take part in the UN peace-keeping actions, in international anti-terror cooperation, and in disaster rescue and relief actions, and play an important role in creating a security environment favorable to the nation's peaceful development. To accomplish the historical mission in the new stage of the

new century, the armed forces must develop the capabilities of coping with various security threats and fulfill diverse military tasks, and should be able to effectively cope with crises, preserve peace, check war, and win war. With the development of the military strategy, there will be major changes in the strategies of various services and arm branches: The army will change from a regional defense pattern to an all-area mobile pattern; the navy will change from a coastal defense pattern to an offshore defense pattern; the air force will change from a homeland air defense pattern to an offensive-and-defensive combination pattern; the Second Artillery will improve its strength system composed of both nuclear and conventional forces. China's self-defense nuclear strategy pursues the nuclear policy of not to be the first to use nuclear weapons, adheres to the principle of self-defensive counterattacks and limited development, and will not get involved in an arms race with any countries.

27. **(III) Strategic Considerations in Adhering to the Defensive National Defense Policy.** In the report to the 17th party national congress, Comrade Hu Jintao once again announced to the world: China will consistently take a path of peaceful development, will pursue a defensive national defense policy, will not engage in any arms race, will not pose military threats against any country; will never seek hegemony, and will never pursue expansion. He explicitly required that the scientific development concept be taken as an important guiding principle for the construction of national defense and the armed forces, and called for quickening the revolution in military affairs with Chinese characteristics, making good preparations for military struggle, and raising the ability of the armed forces to cope with multiple security threats and fulfill diverse military tasks. Comrade Hu Jintao's report to the party congress was of great significance for guiding us to carry out the defensive national defense policy and create a new situation in the construction of national defense and in the building of the armed forces under the new situation. In the new stage of the new century, adhering to the course of peaceful development, striving to build a harmonious society at home and promote the building of a harmonious world externally has become China's basic state policy and state will. All of our strategic considerations and definitions in carrying out the defensive national defense policy must be unfolded closely around the state's peaceful development strategy.

28. First, understand the defensiveness of the national defense policy from the political and strategic high plane. Firmly carrying out the defensive national defense policy is the essential requirement of socialism with Chinese characteristics, and is the inherent requirement of the nature and the principle of the people's armed forces. This comes into line with the state's development strategic and foreign policy, comes into line with the

fundamental interests of the people and the general trend of the world's development, and also comes into line with China's peace-loving cultural tradition and China's characteristics of having a vast territory and a huge population. This is the inevitable choice to be made by China according to the nation's historical experience of suffering from the aggression, plundering, and bullying of foreign powers. Therefore, maintaining the defensiveness of the national defense policy is our political superiority, is our core values, and is an important hallmark of the soft power of our state and our armed forces. Mao Zedong explicitly pointed out that our strategic principle is active defense, and we never strike first. Peng Dehui linked strategic defense and the principle of striking only after being attacked to war as an act of justice. Deng Xiaoping emphasized that even when modernization is realized in the future, we would still pursue strategic defense. All these remarks expressed the profound political significance and values of this tenet. Today, while the Chinese economy is increasingly merging into the global economic system and the state interests are continuously extending outward, China's national defense will assume a more active and open posture in moving into the outside world, will preserve the state interests in a broader sphere of domains beyond the limits of territory and sovereignty, and will provide military support and guarantee for the development of national interests. In such circumstances, we must never repeat the historical track of the Western powers that engaged in overseas expansion and relied on rise with violence by adopting a strategic offensive and preemptive attack principle. Instead, we must unwaveringly adhere to strategic defensiveness, self-defense, and striking only after being attacked. In the long run, this will greatly boost the just and legal nature of our actions to safeguard the state interests, and increase our credibility of taking the course of peaceful development. In a local war under the informatized conditions, the differences between strategic, campaign, and tactical actions are fuzzy; the differences between strategic offensive and strategic defense and between striking only after being attacked and striking preemptively will get narrower. These characteristics require that we more flexibly employ the strategy and tactics, give prominence to the offensive operations at the strategic, campaign, and tactical levels, take active offensive actions to seize the strategic initiative and dominance, effectively safeguard the state's security and development interests. This does not change the defensive nature of our national defense policy, but just enrich and develop the strategic thought of active defense under the premise of adhering to the defensive strategy.

29. Second, it is necessary to establish a scientific security concept with comprehensive security as the core. While facing the comprehensiveness, diversity, and complicatedness of the security threats, the main task of the

state's security strategy is to scientifically plan and preserve the state's comprehensive security, coordinate the relationships between development and security; between internal security and external security; between traditional security and non-traditional security; between homeland security and overseas interests security; and between political security, economic security, military security, and social security. Establishing a scientific security concept with comprehensive security as the core and comprehensively developing and employing the means of national security is the foundation for China's national defense to effectively safeguard the state interests under the new situation. Development and security constitute an organic unified entity, in which development is the foundation for security, and security is the guarantee for development. Being the strong backup for the nation's security and development, national defense should strive to effect the combination of safeguarding both the security interests and the development interests. With China's connection to the outside world changing from a less close condition to a close condition, China's influence on the international community and the external obstruction that China will be facing will rise side by side, so the domestic security will more heavily influence the international situation, and the international security will more deeply influence the domestic situation as well. National defense should coordinate the domestic situation and the international situation, should consider and resolve national security issues from the interactive influence of the international and domestic security factors, and should combine the effort to consolidate the internal security with the effort to guard against the external threats. The traditional security threats with military and political security as the core will continue to exist; at the same time, such non-traditional security threats as those to the economic security, information security, energy security, maritime strategic channel security, public ecological security, and terrorism will continue to rise, and the influence of non-state action entities on the international security will have an impact on the sole status of the state action entities. National defense should grasp the development orientation from the interactive and interwoven connection of the traditional and non-traditional security factors, establish the missions and tasks for the armed forces, attach importance to the non-traditional security while preserving the traditional security. In the front of national security, the anti-separatist, anti-subversion, and anti-containment struggle is complicated and harsh; the task of creating a benign peripheral environment is arduous; with the pace of "stepping out" being quickened, the issue of protecting the overseas interests is getting increasingly prominent. National Defense should, from the high plane of economic globalization's development and safeguarding the state's economic security, effectively raise the capability of protecting our country's overseas interests, and ensure the protection of the overseas interests security while guaranteeing homeland security.

30. Third, it is necessary to attach importance to safeguarding the just and legal nature of the state interests. The international activities aimed at safeguarding the security interests marked by national sovereignty, unity, and territorial integrity are indisputably just in nature. Today, however, while the state's development interests are increasing, the just nature of national defense for safeguarding the state's development interests is facing a challenge. The traditional viewpoint holds that "the physical sphere of national interests is China itself, and it can never be extended to other countries and regions." (Pan Shiying: "Contemporary Strategic Thoughts," p 66, Beijing, Shijie Zhishi Publishing House, 1993) With China's full involvement in the process of economic globalization, the state's development interests will unavoidably go beyond the scope of the country's territory and will certainly be extended to other countries and regions. Therefore, we must pay special attention to safeguarding the just and legal nature of safeguarding the state's development interests. First, we should firmly expand the state interests through peaceful development. The increase in China's comprehensive national power and the development of China's state interests do not come from aggression and expansion abroad, and are not resulted from any hegemony-seeking war, but are the natural result of the peaceful development and competition. China's peaceful development is a process of developing itself through preserving world peace and then promoting world peace through its development. That is, the basic point of development is to mainly rely on its own strength. This thus guarantees the inherent just nature of the development of national interests. Second, we should firmly safeguard our national interests in a cooperative and win-win form. The development of China's interests is closely linked to the development of the common interests of all countries, so the form of safeguarding the state interests must be changed from a closed to open, from zero-sum to win-win, and from passive to active. Only by continuously upholding the new security concept and seeking win-win cooperation, including the international military security cooperation, can we join hands with relevant countries in coping with the non-traditional security threats that particularly affect the state's development interests and thus effectively and justifiably guarantee the sustained development of the state's overseas interests. Finally, we should firmly observe the UN Charter and the generally accepted norms of international relations. To carry out military actions outside the territory for safeguarding the state interests, the armed forces not only need to have good reasons for the actions, but also need to act in accordance with laws, strictly abide by the international cooperation principles of not interfering in other countries'

42

internal affairs and not using threats or violence against other countries as specified by the UN Charter, and observe the international treaties and the bilateral treaties and agreements signed by our state. Only thus can we achieve the strategic objective of safeguarding the state interests and also display our forces' good international image of being peace-loving and civilized.

31. Fourth, it is necessary to adhere to the principles of acting according to our capability and taking an active part in foreign military relations. China is now situated in a special stage of trying to be rich but not being really rich, trying to be strong but not being strong enough, trying to be reunited but not yet realizing national reunification, trying to be stable and not being eventless, trying to become developed but not being fully developed, and undergoing transformations but not completing the transformations. China's external environment is improving, but has not been fundamentally improved. In accordance with the comprehensive consideration of the basic national conditions, the comprehensive national power, and the reality of international power balance, hiding our capabilities and biding our time while making new accomplishments should continue to be the strategic guideline that the state must maintain for a long time. Hiding our capabilities and biding our time is not to passively make concessions, nor to make camouflage and concealment, but to refuse to act as a standard bearer or to claim leadership in the international community, not to make a full display of our power, not to bring trouble to ourselves, avoid becoming the focus of international contradictions, and just concentrate on developing ourselves. To make new accomplishments is to implement the principle of doing things selectively rather than dealing with all things indiscriminately. To safeguard and develop the state interests, we should strive to reduce external disruption and obstruction, properly employ our international influence, and actively play a more constructive role in international affairs. According to this guideline, when handling foreign military relations, we should proceed from the actual conditions of our country and our armed forces, and adhere to the principle of acting according to our capability and active participation. In the building of the armed forces, the principal contradiction is that "the current modernization level is not commensurate with the requirements of winning local war to be fought in informatized conditions, and the military capability is not commensurate with the requirements of the historical mission for our armed forces in the new stage of the new century." ("Readers for Theoretical Study on Establishing and Implementing the Scientific Development Concept," p 201) This determines that we must still adhere to the principle of not acting as a standard bearer, not claim leadership, and undertaking commitments selectively when we take part in international military cooperation; and

that we must deal with different cases in different ways, act according to our capability, and make steady advances in safeguarding and expanding the state interests. When handling the major issues concerning the state's fundamental interests and the fundamental interests of the people in the world, we must hold a clear-cut attitude and be able to do whatever we should do. However, when dealing with ordinary interests issues, we should aim at preserving the overall interests, adopt flexible solutions, and never get involved in the vortex of international contradictions and conflicts. We do not join any military blocs, but we may select various forms for carrying out military cooperation. Only by taking an active part in cooperation can we make accomplishments and keep us in an active and favorable position; only by carrying out extensive cooperation can we relieve pressure and reduce confrontation. The development of national interests requires that we consolidate the control of our land territory, strengthen the sea and air control, develop the control of the electromagnetic domain, the control of information, and the control of outer space. How to prevent us from being regarded as a threat because of development and how to prevent us from being self-restrained in development for fear of being regarded as a threat is a dilemma that we are facing in the development of national defense. Only by creating a benign international environment, enhancing cooperation, seeking win-win results can we effectively and continuously build up our control and superiority in various domains in a way with Chinese characteristics.

32. Fifth, it is necessary to raise the strategic capability of checking crises and wars. The important strategic opportunity period for national development and the overall state interests require that the military strategy aim at the combination of checking war and winning war and the combination of deterrence and real war. Checking and postponing war through various forms, including strategic deterrence, and thus maintaining the strategic stability to the maximum degree is in keeping with the fundamental interests of the state. Winning war is the prerequisite for checking war, but checking war is something more difficult and more complicated and requires a higher level of stratagem employment and greater strategic patience. To check war, we must first actively check and cope with crises. A characteristic of modern warfare is that though the war proper may develop very quickly and last for a shorter period, there is always an obvious stage of crisis outbreak and escalation before the outbreak of the war. A crisis is caused by the intensification of interest conflicts between countries or political groups and is a dangerous state that may lead to various serious consequences, including war. A crisis has the characteristics of being sudden, drastic, threatening, uncertain, and tense. If a crisis can be handled properly, it may be resolved and the situation

may gradually become peaceful; if the crisis goes out of control, then it may escalate and rapidly lead to war. China's security environment is very complicated, and the national security, unity, and development are facing serious challenges. There exist real possibilities of crises and conflicts occurring both in the primary and secondary strategic directions. To achieve the end of checking war and preserving peace, the military strategy must move forward the gravity center of strategic guidance, actively prevent and resolve crises, and resolutely deter the outbreak and escalation of crises. The strategic capability of checking crises and wars mainly includes: First, the strategic prediction capability. Not only do we need to be able to predict the possibility of crisis and war, but we should also be able to issue early warning against any short-term drastic changes. The issuance of early warnings is to make short-term, real-time predictions. It is necessary to establish a sensitive and sound crisis early warning system, promptly analyze and assess changes in security threats, and formulate various plans for preventing and handling crises. This is the prerequisite for preventing and resolving crises. Second, the decision-making and reaction capability. In essence, coping with a crisis is a case of decision-making. That is, while facing a critical scenario of possible outbreak or escalation of a crisis, the decision maker must rapidly make reactions and decisions. Strategic guidance requires that a determination be made as soon as possible to handle an event, and corresponding actions and countermeasures be taken right away, so that various means will be synthetically applied to check the crisis. If necessary, military means should be taken. Third, the deterring and actual combat capability. The basic means of containment is strategic deterrence. It is necessary to build a strategic deterrence system composed of both nuclear and conventional deterring forces, make solid and good preparations for military struggle, flexibly employ various forms of deterrence, give play to the overall effects of integrated national strength and the people's war, and keep strong and firm strategic will and determination. These are the basic conditions for successful deterrence. If a war is unavoidable, then we should dare to achieve our political objective straight away through local and limited operations, prompting peace talks and reconciliation through war, thus ensuring a stable continuation of the important strategic opportunity period and the eventual realization of our strategic goal of building a well-off society in an all-round manner.

On Development of China's Defensive National Defense Policy Under New Situation

By Dr. Chen Zhou, *China Military Science*, (6) 2009 pages 63-71

A full text translation follows.

TEXT:

1. **Abstract:** The development of new China's national defense policy, which is defensive in nature, is closely linked to the changes in the conditions of the times, the security environment, the comprehensive national power, and the war pattern. China's national defense policy is characterized by its self-defense, reactive, peaceful, and active nature. Under the new situation, the basic principles of such defensive policy for national defense will not change, but as new changes have taken place in terms of the scope, task, objective, and means of national defense in safeguarding the national interests, our national defense policy is facing challenges on such major issues as the effectiveness of strategic defense and strategic deterrence, our nation's right of self-defense, and the safeguarding of our nation's overseas interests. We must, according to the new requirements in practice, come up with countermeasures and solutions for dealing with new situations and resolving new issues, and continuously enrich and develop our national defense policy, which is defensive in nature.

2. Under the new situation marked by major changes in the security environment, in the national interests, and in the balance of power, China's nation defense policy, which is defensive in nature, must continue to develop in keeping with the requirement of the times through adding new contents, establishing a new line of thinking, and taking new measures. Deeply analyzing the changes and development of the defensive national defense policy and the new challenges it faces is of great significance to correctly guiding the building and use of the national defense forces and further enriching and improving the military strategic guideline in the new period.

3. **(I) Contents and Grounds of Defensive National Defense Policy.** China's national defense policy is the code of conduct formulated by the state in a specific period for guarding against and resisting aggression, quelling armed subversion, and defending state sovereignty and national security. This policy is the epitome of the state's domestic and foreign policies in the domain of national security. It is a complete system that includes the military strategy of active defense, the nuclear policy of no-first-use of nuclear weapons, the development strategy for the modernization of national defense, the principle and policy for the construction of national

defense and the building of the armed forces, and the arms control and disarmament policy, as well as military-related policies in the aspects of political, economic, diplomatic, scientific and technological, and educational activities. In particular, the military strategy of active defense holds a pivotal and basic position.

4. Before the 1980s, China used the concept of "national defense policy" mainly for introducing the defense and military strategies, the armed forces building notions and policies in the Western countries, and rarely used it to summarize our own relevant policies. The relevant contents of the "national defense policy" were actually embedded in the state's laws, regulations, and foreign policy, and especially in the military strategic guideline of active defense and the concrete policy practice of national defense construction and military struggle. Such a state of affairs was a historical extension of the revolutionary military system and tradition in the years of war, and was also an objective necessity in the long-lasting condition of being ready to resist foreign enemies' large-scale invasion at any time. At the same time, this was also related to the idea that took the term "national defense policy" as a concept in the West. [Footnote: According to relevant data, on 26 November 1982, Jiefangjun Bao for the first time published an article saying that military forecast "may help us formulate a correct national defense policy." On 22 January 1983, Xu Xin (STC: 1776/0207), then deputy chief of general staff, "gave a briefing on our country's national defense policy and the condition of our armed forces building" when giving a banquet in honor of a visiting delegation of the Royal Military College of Canada. In March 1986, the PLA General Staff Department held a series of forums on national defense modernization, and one of the lectures was entitled "China's Ancient Military Strategies and National Defense Policies." On 30 May 1987, Zhang Aiping, then minister of national defense, gave a briefing on "China's national defense policy" when meeting with the visiting chief of Japan's Defense Agency, stressing that "China carries out the policy of active defense, and will not encroach on an inch of foreign territory, but we will neither allow other countries to encroach on an inch of our territory." In the early 1990s, some scholars held that China's notion of "national defense policy" was the same as, or similar to, the notions of "national defense policy" or "defense policy" in the Western countries.] However, no matter in what forms the concrete contents of the national defense policy are expressed, it is always the guideline for directing and regulating all national defense activities of the state.

5. In the early period after the founding of new China, China already announced its defensive national defense policy to the world. The "Common Outline of the CPPCC" passed in 1949 stipulated that the task

of China's national defense was to "defend China's independence and the integrity of its territory and sovereignty, and defend the Chinese people's revolution achievements and all legitimate rights and interests." The "PRC Constitution" enacted in 1954 stipulated that the task of the Chinese armed forces was to "defend the achievements of the people's revolution and the nation's building, defend state sovereignty, territorial integrity, and national security." At that time, the contents of China's defensive national defense policy mainly included the following: consolidating national defense, resisting aggression, defending state sovereignty, territorial integrity, and security; upholding the principle of active defense and attack only after being attacked; being ready for responding to sudden incidents and large-scale foreign invasions; building the national defense forces by mainly relying on our own efforts; organizing all people's defense on the basis of turning every citizen into a soldier; and maintaining the leadership of the CPC over national defense.

6. Along with the great historical process of reform and opening up, major changes have taken place in China's national defense policy. In the 1998 "China's National Defense" white paper, China, for the first time, summarized five main points of its national defense policy in the form of a government document: consolidate national defense, resist aggression, quell armed subversion, defend state sovereignty, national unity, territorial integrity, and security; national defense construction will be subordinate to and serve the overall interests of national economic construction; implement the military strategic guideline of active defense; take the course of building elite forces with Chinese characteristics; safeguard world peace, and oppose all acts of aggression and expansion. The "2000 China's National Defense" white paper increased the contents of the national defense policy to seven points, that is, adding the points of "building and consolidating national defense independently and self-reliantly" and "effecting military-civilian integration and all-people self-defense." The "2006 China's National Defense" white paper, with the scientific development concept as the grounds, comprehensively and systematically enunciated China's defensive national defense policy at the new stage in the new century. The main contents of this policy are: maintain national security and unity, safeguard the national development interests; effect the comprehensive, coordinated, and sustainable development of national defense and armed forces building; strengthen the armed forces' quality building with informatization as the main hallmark; implement the military strategic guideline of active defense; adhere to the nuclear strategy of self-defensive defense; and create a security environment that is conducive to the nation's peaceful development.

7. From an in-depth examination of the "defensive" nature of China's national defense policy, one may sum up the following characteristics: First,

the self-defensive nature. The fundamental objective and task of national defense is self-defense, rather than launching a war, carrying out aggression and expansion, or entering into an arms race. The starting point and the foothold of China's national defense is to resist aggression, defend the motherland, and defend the people's peaceful work, while strictly adhering to the position of self-defense militarily. The modernization of national defense is based on the needs of national security and development, and the notions of the people's war and all-people self-defense are upheld. The self-defensive nature of the national defense policy comes into line with the steadfastness of defending the national interests. This is precisely the case that "we will not attack unless we are attacked; if we are attacked, we will certainly counterattack."

8. Second, the character of being reactive to attack. A pivotal point in the defensive nature of China's national defense policy is the strategic character of overpowering the adversary by means of counteroffensive after being attacked. Mao Zedong pointed out: China's strategic principle is active defense, and China will never take preemptive action. Peng Dehuai (STC: 1756/1795/2037) pointed out: Even if we have discovered that the enemy will soon stage large-scale attacks on our country, we still cannot be the first to fight into the territory of the hostile country; otherwise, we will lose the righteousness of war. [Footnote: see "Selected Military Works by Peng Dehuai," p 590, Beijing, Contemporary China Publishing House, 1993] The fundamental purpose of China's policy of not being the first to use nuclear weapons and its self-defensive nuclear strategy is to keep other countries from using or threatening to use nuclear weapons against China. This gives full expression to the self-defensive nature of our national defense policy.

9. Third, the peace-oriented character. The core of China's foreign policy is to strive for world peace. Striving for peace and try to postpone the outbreak of war as much as possible is also the fundamental objective of our national defense policy with a defensive nature. The 1949 "CPPCC Common Outline" and the 1954 "PRC Constitution" both emphasized that China's unswerving principle was to "endeavor for the lofty objective of world peace and human progress." The national defense policy implements the state's foreign policy, adheres to the five principles of peaceful coexistence, opposes aggression policy and war policy, and supports all activities that are conducive to world and regional peace, security, and stability.

10. Fourth, the nature of activeness. The fundamental character of the national defense policy is to serve the purpose of defense rather than being offensive. However, in terms of military strategy, such defense should not be passive or purely defensive, but should be active defense

based on the combination of offensive and defensive operations, which is a combination of strategic defense with offensive campaigns and battles, or a combination of strategic defense with strategic counteroffensive and strategic offensive. Such activeness means that before the outbreak of a war, efforts are made by all means to check or postpone the outbreak of the war; and during the war, operational and tactical actions are actively taken to smash the enemy's attacks, and efforts are also made to seek international political and economic aid to safeguard peace and check the war. [Footnote: see "Selected Military Works by Peng Dehuai," pp 588-589]

11. In the years of revolutionary wars, the strategy of active defense was the strategic principle of the people's army, and was also the general strategic guideline for China's revolutionary wars. This was mainly determined by the comparison of power between our forces and the stronger enemies. The defensive national defense policy established by new China maintained the military strategy of active defense. This was no longer aimed at dealing with the situation in which our forces were weaker and the enemy forces were stronger, but was closely related to our state system, the security environment, and the changes in the war pattern. These new historical conditions were also the basic grounds for determining the defensive nature of our national defense policy.

12. The conditions were greatly different between the period of the democratic revolution and the period of socialist revolution and construction. The establishment of the socialist system marked the greatest and most profound change in China's history. According to the principle that military affairs must be subordinate to political needs, the character of our national defense policy and military strategy should first be determined by the socialist nature of the state and its policies. At the enlarged meeting of the Central Military Commission in March 1956 and at the plenary meeting of the National Defense Committee in July 1957, Peng Dehuai gave a representative explanation to the defensive nature of our strategic guideline: China is a socialist country with a system of the people's democracy, and has eliminated the private ownership of the means of production and the bourgeois class which piles up a fortune by means of war and plundering colonies, so China will not produce any elements of invading other countries; China's current general task is to strive for a peaceful international environment that will last for a fairly long period and to build a great socialist country, so China does not need to launch a war against any other countries; China's peaceful foreign policy calls for establishing state-to-state relations on the basis of the five principles of peaceful coexistence and settling international disputes by means of negotiations rather than by means of war. "Our country's nature, task, and foreign policy all clearly show that our strategic principle can only

be defensive in nature." [Footnote: see "Selected Works by Peng Dehuai," p 588]

13. In a long period after the found of new China, the existence of the actual threats of large-scale foreign aggression and the strategic situation in which the enemy forces were more powerful than ours continued to be the main consideration in deciding the defensive nature of our national defense policy. In the 1950s, the strategic principle of active defense was based on the consideration of responding to the possible sudden strategic attacks by the armed forces headed by the US forces on China's eastern coastal area. In the mid-1960s, the United States and the Soviet Union both became the main strategic opponents, and the main strategic directions were the eastern coastal area and the northern border areas. In the early 1970s, the Soviet Union became the main operation opponent, and the main strategic directions were pointed to the northeast, northern, and northwest border areas. In all those periods, the strategic guideline was always based on defeating enemies with superior armaments under the most complicated and most difficult conditions. In September 1980, in a proposal on the strategic principle, Song Shilun (STC: 1345/2514/6544) pointed out: "The strategic principle of active defense is determined by the socialist system of our country and by the feature in which the enemies have more powerful technology and armaments than us." [Footnote: see "Selected Military Works by Song Shilun," p 242, Beijing, Military Science Press, 2007] Therefore, in a fairly long period after the founding of new China, the strategic principle of active defense, in general, still followed the same strategic guiding thinking in the years of revolutionary wars.

14. The change of the war pattern and especially the change in the approach to the role of nuclear weapons in war became an important ground for the establishment of the defensive national defense policy with being reactive to attack as the core. In the mid-1950s, the Soviet Union began to pursue a preemptive strategic principle, and changed its strategy from "strengthening active defense, preventing enemy aggression" into a rocket-nuclear strategy, with emphasis on the first-strike role of nuclear weapons. In response to this change, at a meeting of the CPC Central Secretariat in late April 1955, Mao Zedong particularly emphasized that China would adhere to the principle of active defense and never be the first to attack. In May 1955, Peng Dehuai attended a conference of the Warsaw Pact countries in the capacity of observer, and there he expounded China's principle of active defense and not being the first to attack. [Footnote: see "The Biography of Peng Dehuai," pp 535-536] Mao Zedong also mentioned on multiple occasions: Both world wars ended up with the victory of the defending side and the failure of the attacking side. Things developed by the Soviet advisers (operation plans and scenarios)

are all offensive in nature, and have no defense, so they are not in keeping with the actual conditions. In the future, we will produce a small quantity of nuclear weapons, but we do not intend to use them, and will just use them for the defensive purpose. Mao Zedong always held that what determined the outcome of a war was not atomic bombs or advanced technology and equipment, but the nature of war and the trend of popular sentiment. This was also an important reason why China dared to adhere to the strategy of active defense in any circumstances.

15. **(II) New Changes and New Contents in Defensive National Defense Policy.** Today, the historical process of reform and opening up in China has entered a new stage of national peaceful development and interest expansion, and is situated in an important strategic opportunity period in national development. In the world today, peace and development remains the theme of the times, the world's multi-polar trend and economic globalization are developing in an in-depth manner, the interdependent interest relationship between various countries keeps deepening, and changes in the growth and decline of international strategic forces are quickening. It is unlikely that a major war will break out in a fairly long period to come, but security threats are getting increasingly more comprehensive, more diverse, and more complicated. For China today, there is no real danger of a large-scale foreign invasion, but the complex intermingling and interaction of various security threats and challenges and the rise of its comprehensive national power and international influence will inevitably change the contents and the existence forms of national interests, with the issue of development emerging as one that affects the overall situation of national security.

16. Under the new historical conditions, should we continue to uphold the defensive national defense policy? The answer is yes. Persistently pursuing the national defense policy with a defensive nature, which naturally comes with socialism with Chinese characteristics and the nature and aim of the people's army, is the essential requirement of our country's peaceful development strategy and foreign policy, as well as the inevitable option based on China's historical experience of suffering from foreign powers' aggression, pillage, and bullying. Therefore, this is our political advantage and our core values, as well as an important hallmark of the soft power of our state and military. In the long run, upholding this policy will greatly strengthen the righteousness and legitimacy of our effort to safeguard our national interests, and increase our credibility of taking the course of peaceful development.

17. At the same time, it should also be noted that with changes in the conditions of the times, the security environment, and the comprehensive national power, although the basic principle of the defensive national

defense policy will remain unchanged, new changes have taken place in terms of its contents and expression form.

18. First, the expansion of the scope. National interests are the fundamental grounds for the formulation of national defense policy and military strategy. The traditional viewpoint holds that the range and space of national interests is China's territory itself and can never be extended to other countries and regions. Under the new situation marked by the change of the times and our national development, with the intermingling of the security interests and development interests and with the close connection between our country's interests and other countries' interests, the gravity center of interests has shifted from survival to development, the form of realization has shifted from domestic to international, and the range of existence has expanded from the traditional domains of territorial land, territorial sea, and territorial airspace to the oceans, outer space, and electromagnetic sphere. The development interests have become the core of national interests. With China's economy being merged into the global economic system, while facing the increasingly intense geo-strategic rivalry of the big powers and the prolonged existence of the external strategic pressure, outward expansion of national interests is inevitable, and our national defense needs to safeguard the national interests and seize the strategic initiative in a broader sphere beyond our territory where we exercise sovereignty. As early as October 1950, when talking about the principle and plan for entering Korea to take on military operations, Mao Zedong put forth the notion of "national defense line," that is, "the national defense line should be pushed forward from Yalujiang River to Tokchon, Nyongwon, and further south, and this is what we are able to do and is also greatly beneficial." [Footnote: Mao Zedong: "Telegram to Zhou Enlai on the Principle and Plan for the Chinese Volunteers' Operations in Korea," in "Party Documents," 2000 (No. 5), p 8] In 1965, Liu Bocheng (STC: 0491/0130/2110) also said that the Navy should have a broader vision and should go beyond the limits of China's inshore waters. In the 1980s, the sphere of China's strategic defense was shifted from the deep interior areas to surrounding regions, and the Navy's strategy was shifted from inshore defense to offshore defense. Today, while major changes are going on in the strategic situation and in our comprehensive national power, in implementing the strategy of active defense, we should break through the limits of China's coastline, and actively construct strategic buttresses in surrounding regions, expand the defense forward positions, stretch the "national defense line" in the sea and in the air, adjust the strategic layout, and seize the strategic commanding heights.

19. Second, the expansion of the objective. The fundamental objective of national defense is precisely to guard against and resist aggression,

quell armed subversion, and defend the nation's security, unity, and development interests. Under the new situation, the fundamental objective of national defense remains unchanged, but new contents are added to the objectives of concrete strategic actions: First, from winning wars to checking wars. In the past, the national defense policy and the military strategy were mainly aimed at winning wars, and were mainly based on preparing for and conducting war efforts. Today, the important strategic opportunity period for national development and overall national interests require that checking wars be taken as the primary objective of the military strategy and that unity between checking wars and winning wars be achieved. The capability of winning wars is the prerequisite for checking wars, but it is more difficult to successfully check the outbreak of wars, as such efforts will be facing more complicated conditions, and require a higher stratagem level and greater strategic patience. To successfully keep wars in check, it is necessary to actively cope with crises. China is facing a complicated security environment, and it is possible that in reality, crises and conflicts occur in the primary and secondary strategic directions. As far as the military strategy is concerned, we must move forward the gravity center of strategic guidance to prevent and check crises, conflicts, and wars in various forms and by various means, including strategic deterrence to maintain strategic stability to the maximum extent. Second, from striving for peace to preserving peace. In a fairly long period in the past, an important objective of the national defense policy was to check or defer the outbreak of a new world war and a full-scale war of aggression against China, and to strive to prolong the peacetime as much as possible. In the new epoch with peace and development as the main theme, the possibility of a world war can basically be ruled out, and the fundamental interests of our nation are focused on economic construction and the enhancement of comprehensive national power. Safeguarding our nation's peaceful development and safeguarding world peace have become the basic objective of our national defense policy. Deng Xiaoping said: China's national interests lie in two points, one is to shake off poverty, and the other is to safeguard peace. [Footnote: see "Outline for the Study of Deng Xiaoping's Thinking on Armed Forces Building in the New Period," compiled by the PLA General Political Department, p 21; Beijing, PLA Press, 1997] The national defense policy should put the safeguarding of the nation's security, unity, and development interests in the top position, and also should try as much as possible to avoid, or not to get involved in, external wars, especially avoiding all-out confrontations with the world's major powers by keeping China's security frictions with other big powers to a low intensity and under control.

20. Third, the expansion of the task. Safeguarding national interests is the fundamental task of national defense and the fundamental function of the armed forces. At the new stage in the new century, national defense should put the task of safeguarding state sovereignty, security, territorial integrity, guaranteeing the national development interests, and protecting the people's interests in a paramount position above everything else, and safeguard the important strategic opportunity period, to ensure that the building of a well-off society is carried out without a hitch. To safeguard national interests under the new situation, it is necessary to take the scientific development concept as the guide and the composite security concept as the basis. Development and security constitute an organic integrated entity. National defense should bear in mind the overall situation of national security and the development strategy, strive to realize the unity of state sovereignty, national security, and development interests, and strive for the nation's comprehensive political, economic, military, and social security. China has never been so closely tied up with the world. Our national defense should be closely brought into line with both the domestic situation and the international situation, in such a way that national security issues are considered and tackled amid the interaction between the domestic and external factors to achieve the unity of consolidating internal security and guarding against external threats. Different security threats and challenges exist in our country's different strategic directions. While continuing to step up military struggle preparations in the primary strategic direction, national defense should also push for the coordinated development of military struggle preparations in other strategic directions, and safeguard the maritime security, ground security, and air security. Traditional security threats still exist, all kinds of separatist forces' activities are running wild, and such nontraditional threats as terrorism, natural disasters, and the threats to the security of energy resources and strategic channels continue to increase. As far as national defense is concerned, we should grasp the development direction from the intermingling of traditional and nontraditional security factors, and raise the armed forces' capability of coping with various security threats and fulfilling diversified military tasks. The state is quickening the implementation of the "going global" strategy, and the issue of protecting our nation's overseas interests has become increasingly prominent. National defense should, from the high plane of safeguarding national development interests and protecting the people's interests, earnestly raise the capability of protecting overseas interests, and maintain the security of overseas interests while ensuring homeland security.

21. Fourth, the expansion of the means. Along with the expansion of national interests, and changes in the objective and task of national

defense, our country is still facing prolonged, complicated, and multiple security threats and challenges, which have set even higher requirements for the use of the military power. The national defense policy must ensure the flexible use of various military struggle forms in dealing with different security threats, strengthen the activeness and initiative in the use of military means, closely cooperate with the use of the political, economic, diplomatic, cultural, and legal means in serving national security and the development strategy and achieving comprehensive national security. The military strategy should focus on enhancing the actual war fighting capability under informatized conditions, step up the construction of a strategic deterrence power system, and create effective deterrence against adversaries. The important links of raising the strategic deterring capability include continuing to strengthen military struggle preparations, accelerating the development of strategic projection and intermediate-range and long-range precision striking capabilities, carrying military deterring actions, small-scale warning operations, and other preventive actions in good time, actively and prudently making strategic pre-deployment, and giving play to the overall efficacy of the comprehensive national power and the people's war. Against the general background of the intermingling of traditional and nontraditional security threats and the intermingling of domestic and international security issues, it is necessary to, from the high plane of the overall long-term and strategic interests, deeply understand the necessity and urgency of using military forces to deal with nontraditional security issues. Non-war military actions have extensive contents, diverse forms, and the characteristics of low intensity, high efficiency, being limited in scope, and strong controllability, and thus greatly expand the room for strategic maneuvering. Therefore, non-war military actions should be taken as a major form whereby the nation's military forces are used, and should be planned and carried out from the high plane of strategy. We should take an active part in UN peace-keeping operations, international counterterrorism cooperation, and international disaster rescue and relief operations, take the initiative in promoting international military security cooperation, strengthen military diplomatic activities, conduct military exchanges in various forms, and push for the establishment of military mutual trust mechanisms. The arms control and disarmament policy should be consistently included in the national defense policy. Importance should be attached, and support should be given, to the international arms control, disarmament, and anti-proliferation efforts to give full expression to the defensive nature of China's national defense policy and our determination to take the course of peaceful development.

22. **(III) Thoughts on Several Issues on Implementation of Defensive National Defense Policy.** Under the new historical conditions, as far as the

implementation of the defensive national defense policy is concerned, we are facing many new circumstances, new issues, and new challenges. Some of the previous practice and experience are no longer completely applicable, so we must continue to emancipate the mind and keep blazing new trails and making innovations according to the new practical requirements, and come up with countermeasures and methods that are commensurate with the new situation and help resolve the new issues.

23. First, strategic defense and strategic offensive. As far as the national defense policy at the new stage in the new century is concerned, we should continue to adhere to the principle of strategic defense, self-defense, attacking only after being attacked, be prudent in the use of force, and "never fire first" in strategic terms. However, the new situation requires that prominence be given to the initiative and the offensive character of the military strategic actions, and this adds new substance to the strategic notion of attacking only after being attacked. How to handle the relationship between strategic defense and strategic offensive is an important issue in the national defense policy with a defensive nature. From the perspective of the relationship between the end and the means, the defensive character based on a self-defensive strategy and centered at counterattacks after being attacked gives expression to the political objective and political nature of the national defense policy and the military strategy, and active and flexible military actions are the means of achieving this end. In the past, over a long period, we oriented preparedness to fighting large-scale wars against strategically more powerful enemies. Then, strategic defense was the political end and also the means of operations, and the two sides were unified. Today, while striving to win local wars under informatized conditions and safeguard our nation's peaceful development, as our national power and military might have substantially enhanced and the status of traditional defensive operations declined, the political characteristic of strategic defense has become more outstanding and given more prominent expression to the essential nature of the state's political strategy, that is, the state's fundamental system and task, basic policy, and development strategy, and strategic defensive operation is just one of the multiple military means. In such circumstances, the core of strategic defense is to politically pursue the defensive strategy and militarily adhere to the self-defensive position to achieve the fundamental objective of safeguarding state sovereignty, unity, and development interests, while persistently maintaining the principle of not carrying out aggression, not seeking hegemony, and not pursuing military expansion. In future wars, such strategic defensive action patterns as strategic anti-air-raid operations and strategic anti-blockade operations will still hold an important position, but compared with the situation in the early stage of a war in the past,

in which priority, in terms of strategic and campaign-level guidance, was mainly given to defensive operations, things are quite different, because such defensive operations are just a component part of the whole offensive and defense system. The requirements of military struggle for safeguarding national security, unity, and development interests, the informatized operations that are characterized by the blurred delimitation of different types of actions and by the rising status of offensive operations, and the fact that it can hardly distinguish a "preemptive" action from a "reactive" action in strategic information warfare and other strategic actions all indicate the necessity of attaching great importance to the strategic use of offensive operations, to the notion of giving prominence to offensive in strategic actions, and to the seizure of the strategic initiative through effective offensive operations. After the outbreak of a war, we should strive to directly achieve the political objective through active offensives at the strategic, campaign, and tactical levels; we should seize the strategic and campaign-level gravity center in the first battle for fighting decisively, and strive to win the whole war as soon as possible; and we should resolutely carry out strategic actions on exterior lines and strive to wipe out the enemy forces in areas far away from us. In the handling of the new situation in military struggle, we have grasped certain initiative in determining the timing, forms, and targets of the operations. As the actions of splitting the motherland or infringing upon our sovereignty and our national rights and interests occur first, we can secure the righteousness and legitimacy of our actions on the basis of the domestic laws and relevant international laws. Therefore, we must correctly handle the relationship, in connection with the overall political and strategic situation, of not being the first to attack and strive to seize the initiative in strategic actions, firmly establish the strategic awareness of preempting the adversary, and strengthen the initiative in and the flexibility of strategic guidance.

24. Second, the effectiveness of strategic deterrence and the nuclear policy of no-first-use of nuclear weapons. The nuclear policy of no-first-use of nuclear weapons is the core of the defensive national defense policy. Its essence is that China will not be the first to use nuclear weapons at any time and in any circumstances; China unconditionally promises that it will not use or threaten to use nuclear weapons against nuclear-free countries and regions; and China stands for completely prohibiting and thoroughly destroying nuclear weapons. Profound changes took place in the nuclear strategic posture of the world after the end of the Cold War. For example, the US-Russian nuclear strategic balance was shaken; the United States sped up the development of the missile defense system, and included China in the target countries for its possible nuclear strikes; and nuclear proliferation and nuclear hot spots increased in our peripheral areas. This

has increased the nuclear pressure on China, and the effectiveness of our nuclear deterrence is facing a stern challenge. Some people in the academic circle have proposed that under the new situation, continuing to pursue this policy will weaken China's nuclear deterrence, especially when China is facing an adverse situation in which its crucial interests are being jeopardized. To view from the high plane of the overall political and strategic interests, we must remain committed unconditionally to the position of not being the first to use nuclear weapons and maintain the stability and continuity of our nuclear policy. First, this is conducive to the realization of strategic deterrence. "No first use of nuclear weapons" means that nuclear weapons will be taken as the last resort of self-defensive operations, and the role of nuclear weapons is limited to deterring the adversary from launching nuclear attacks. This fully manifests the defensive purpose of China's nuclear weapon development, and also greatly increases the credibility of China's nuclear deterrence, which can effectively play a strategic deterring role against nuclear threats and nuclear attacks. Not being the first to use nuclear weapons is not equivalent to not using nuclear weapons at all. When our country suffers nuclear attacks, we must resolutely deal retaliatory nuclear counterattacks on the adversary. From the angle of deterrence, if the precondition for "being the first to use nuclear weapons" is set vaguely, this will actually lower the credibility of deterrence. If other people do not believe that we may be the first to use nuclear weapons, then the deterring effect will just be zero; if other people do not believe that we will not be the first to use nuclear weapons, then the deterrence will be effective. Some Western powers do not believe that we will adhere to this policy in any circumstances, and this objectively achieves the purpose of deterrence. Second, this is a feasible policy. Nuclear weaponry should be the last option. Our current policy is a policy under normal conditions. The policy of no-first-use of nuclear weapons provides us with great room for maneuver in normal times. This policy requires that nuclear weapons must have strong survival capability and great penetration capability, and should be able to launch counterattacks after suffering nuclear attacks. Actually, this sets forth an urgent requirement for modernizing China's nuclear weapons. If the promise of not being the first to use nuclear weapons is not unconditional, then this means in certain conditions, China might be the first to use nuclear weapons. Such a policy would have no feasibility, because the "conditions" for not being the first to use nuclear weapons must be clearly laid down first. The United States talked a lot about its preemptive strikes, but kept its "deliberate fuzziness" on when and under what conditions it would use nuclear weapons. In addition, not being the first to use nuclear weapons also helps prevent nuclear confrontation caused by misjudgments on accidental and unexpected events. Third, we may gain great political benefits from this policy. Not being the first to use nuclear weapons is, in the first place, a political consideration. It is a policy, and also a strategic thought, a philosophical notion, and a cultural tradition. It is a way of securing the righteousness and legitimacy of possessing nuclear weapons on the basis of deeply understanding the nature of nuclear weapons and China's true advantages. Therefore, the policy of not being the first to use nuclear weapons established by the revolutionary leaders of the older generation is full of wisdom, and is the best option for a country that possesses comparatively fewer nuclear weapons to exercise nuclear deterrence.

25. Third, the state's self-defense right and the principle of non-interference in other countries' internal affairs. National defense activities aimed at safeguarding state sovereignty, national unity, and territorial integrity have unquestionable righteousness and legitimacy. However, with the increase and outward extension of national development interests, how to safeguard the continuingly expanding national interests while adhering to the principle of non-interference in other countries' internal affairs has become a major challenge to the defensive national defense policy. The "Charter of the United Nations" gives countries the right to use force for self-defense. According to Article 51 of the "Charter of the United Nations," it is legal to use force for self-defense in international relations, either standalone self-defense or collective self-defense. However, how to comprehend the state's self-defense right is controversial in the circle of international jurists. Some people hold that a country can exercise the self-defense right while being attacked by force, and can also exercise the self-defense right for such reasons as protecting its national's life and property rights, or the nation's political and economic independence. Some people maintain that being attacked by force is the sole condition for exercising the self-defense right; otherwise, various countries will be indirectly encouraged to take actions in violation of the principle of the UN Charter in the name of exercising the self-defense right. This is actually a legitimacy issue for a country's self-defense right in protecting its overseas interests. Whether or not a country can effectively protect its overseas interests is an issue that directly affects its domestic and external image and its international standing, but is also a very sensitive issue as it involves the sovereign interests of the host countries. In history, before World War I, the international community generally recognized the legitimacy of using force to protect overseas nationals' life and property safety. After the "Charter of the United Nations" took effect in 1945, some Western countries continued to maintain that using force to protect their overseas nationals is legal self-defense. In the past, we completely equated this with aggression and interference in other countries' internal affairs. This had something to do with the historical conditions of our country's relatively closed status and

relatively weak power. Along with the development of reform and opening up and the growth of our comprehensive national power, we inevitably have to safeguard the safety of energy resources supply and the transportation passages and protect the legal rights and interests of Chinese nationals and legal persons in overseas areas and the legitimate rights and interests of overseas Chinese nationals, and must take this as an important part of national security. This is the state's right and power, as well as the state's responsibility and obligation. Moreover, the overseas interests of contemporary China are based on the five principles of peaceful coexistence, and are completely different from the Western powers' interests that were obtained through wars and unequal treaties in the past, so ours are of true legality and legitimacy. [Footnote: Some scholars hold that China's overseas interests refer to China's national interests that are produced by the Chinese government, enterprises, social organizations, and citizens through their global connections, exist beyond China's sovereignty and jurisdiction mainly in the form of international contracts. Such overseas interests include those exist within other countries' sovereignty and jurisdiction, and also include those exist in the international public activity space, and they can be divided into different levels as core interests, important interests, and marginal interests. See "On China's Overseas Interests" by Su Changhe in "Shijie Jingji Yu Zhengzhi," [World Economics and Politics] 2009 (No. 8), pp 13, 15; "Diplomatic Management of National Overseas Interests Risks" by Zhang Shuguang in "Shijie Jingji Yu Zhengzhi," 2009 (No. 8), p 7] In the 21st century, a notion of "sovereign rights based on responsibilities," which emphasizes that sovereign rights include both rights and responsibilities," has posed a challenge to the traditional concept of sovereignty. After the publishing of the "Outcome Document" of the UN Summit in September 2005, the notion that states shoulder responsibility for their people and for the international community became a consensus. [Footnote: See "Predicament of Overseas Nationals Protection and Way Out" by Wan Xia in "Shijie Jingji Yu Zhengzhi," 2005 (No. 5), p 39] Therefore, though we resolutely oppose "neo-interventionism" that "puts human rights above sovereignty," we cannot negate the overseas use of military power for any self-defensive and humanitarian purposes. We must reserve our right to carry out legal "intervention" or "interference' when our nation's core overseas interests are being seriously jeopardized. [Footnote: Some scholars came up with such concepts as "new-non-interventionism," "constructive intervention," or "positive intervention." See "The High Ground of China's Diplomacy" by Wang Yizhou, pp 44, 73, Beijing, China Social Sciences Press, 2008; "On China's Overseas Interests" by Su Changhe in "Shijie Jingji Yu Zhengzhi," 2008 (No. 8), p 19.] We should take the norms of international relations stipulated by the "Charter of the United Nations" and accepted generally by the international community as the grounds, uphold and develop the principle of non-interference in internal affairs of other countries, adhere to the principle of getting the consent of the territory-owning countries and being based on international cooperation, and take military actions according to law to protect our nation's overseas interests within the UN collective security framework.

26. Fourth, safeguarding overseas national interests and not setting up military bases in overseas areas. Military capability is the core of national strategic capabilities, and the strong support for other forms of safeguarding national interests. The functions and missions of the armed forces should stretch to wherever the national interests are expanded to. To safeguard the continuously expanding national strategic interests, we must strengthen the strategic capabilities of the armed forces and enhance the strategic pre-deployment. The new requirement of the national security strategy poses a challenge to the traditional notion of not dispatching one single soldier outside the country and not setting up any overseas military base. Since the 1990s, to perform the international duty of safeguarding peace and promoting development, our military has changed the practice from not taking part in UN peace-keeping actions to sending observers and then dispatching organic military units to take part in such actions, and has also gotten involved in international anti-terrorism cooperation and disaster relief activities, and carried out multilateral or bilateral joint military exercises with foreign militaries. This, in reality, has broken through the limitation of not dispatching and using military forces in overseas areas. As for whether or not military bases should be established in overseas areas, this is something related to our country's independent peaceful foreign policy and defensive national defense policy, and is also restricted by the national and military conditions, the comprehensive national power, and the path of development in our country. The political principle of not seeking hegemony, not entering into alliance, and not pursuing military expansion and the national strategy of peaceful development determine that we will not, and have no need to, take the old path of the Western powers in expanding and preserving overseas interests. China is a large developing country that is getting richer but not affluent yet, and getting stronger but not powerful yet. We must adhere to the strategic principle of hiding our capacities and biding our time for making accomplishments over a long time. China's "going global" strategy is driven by economic interests and based on the principle of equal competition, and, in terms of geopolitics, mainly gives prominence to the presence of its economic power. These conditions and characteristics and the fact that our military's strategic capabilities are not yet commensurate with the requirement of the missions determine that we should act within our capacity in safeguarding our overseas interests, deal with issues case by case, and make steady advances. In a fairly long period to come, the non-war form will continue

to be the main form of safeguarding our overseas interests. Even when we become really powerful in the future, we will still not establish a global network of military bases and station forces in overseas areas on a large scale like some countries do to give accompanying protection for the national overseas interests. Therefore, we should continue to emancipate the mind, seek truth from facts, actively explore the forms and methods of carrying out our military's overseas military actions, and attach great importance to the non-war use of the armed forces, especially the Navy. We should more quickly raise the armed forces' rapid response, strategic delivery, and comprehensive support capabilities, to ensure that the armed forces can rapidly maneuver within our country's territorial land, territorial sea, and territorial airspace, and can also perform diversified military tasks in a broader domain. We should expand the sphere of maritime activity, strive to demonstrate our presence in some critical strategic regions, use diplomatic and economic means to establish strategic supporting points, and make use of berthing points and supply points to which we legally get access from relevant countries in the relevant sea areas. We should, according to the strategic requirement of getting needed support, explore new forms of military security cooperation beyond the scope of general exchange. We should quicken the pace of establishing a legal system for foreign military actions, enlarge the scale and intensity of participating in multilateral military actions, and dispatch organic combat units to take part in the United Nations' peace-keeping actions. All this will not change the nature of China's national defense policy, but will just enrich and develop the defensive national defense policy on the premise of strategic defense, self-defense, and attacking only after being attacked.